Allergy-Free
Cooking
Everyone *Loves*

301 recipes so good you won't know what's missing!

By Stephanie Hapner

MOUNTZ
MEDIA & PUBLISHING

ISBN 978-0-9840673-2-9
Allergy-Free Cooking Everyone Loves
301 Recipes So Good You Won't Know What's Missing

Published by Mountz Media & Publishing
P.O. Box 702398
Tulsa, Oklahoma 74170-2398
918.296.0995
www.mountzmedia.com

For reader convenience, some of the recipes contained in *Allergy-Free Cooking Everyone Loves* are reprinted from the author's first cookbook, *So, What do You Eat?* printed in the United States, 2007, ISBN 12-978-1-4243-3697-5.

Disclaimer: These recipes were created as a tool to help people with food allergies or sensitivities. They are not a cure for symptoms or conditions, but may be helpful to some who use them. Ingredient food labels should be read thoroughly each time an item is purchased because food companies are known to change product contents without informing consumers. No information contained in this book is meant to replace a doctor's instruction. Readers are always advised to check with their physician before making any substantial dietary changes; especially readers who are pregnant, younger than 18 years of age or who have other conditions that compromise their health. Most of the recipes included are wheat, dairy, gluten, peanut and corn free with no use of refined sugars, and each recipe is coded to show which allergens it does not contain. These codes are to be used as a convenience tool and guide only. Due to manufacturer's changes, product selection and human error, we cannot guarantee that the finished product resulting from any included recipe is free of each ingredient in which it is coded. We've done our very best to provide a quality product, but we cannot guarantee that by using these recipes readers will avoid any or all allergic or sensitivity reactions; ultimate responsibility must rest with the reader and his or her doctor.

Contents

Acknowledgements

Dedication

I dedicate this creative endeavor to my husband, Brad, whose continued support and encouragement inspired me to keep working on new things and taking on new projects. Brad, without your strength and love, this book would not be possible.

I also dedicate this book to my son, Wesley. Thank you for remaining strong through the journey life has given you. Because of your journey God has revealed the gift He has so graciously given me. Perhaps your strength and willingness to share your story will enable many other kids to endure and triumph as well.

I love you both so very much.

"And we know that in all things God works for the good of those who love him and are called according to his purpose." ~ Romans 8:28 (NIV)

Thanks to my family for believing in me and encouraging me to share what I've learned so others can benefit.

Thanks to Wanda Cullison for encouraging me to compile my recipes in book form and for the nutrition education she's given me over the past few years.

Thanks to Bruce Helvie for his gracious gift and talented photography.

Thanks to Pam Gregory for her help through the years.

Thanks to Becca Hayes and Hope Beezely for helping with food artistry.

Thanks to David and Marah Grant and Memory Lane Photography for production and photography assistance and use of equipment.

Thanks to Mike and Deonda Jones for willing hands to serve often and in any way possible.

And a **special thanks** to Jon, Stephanie and Megan; Mike and Ella; Zack, Nathyn and Johl; Justin and Sara; Alan and Michele; Heather; Justin; Dan and Robin; Susan and Steve; Lisa; John; Rene; Jen and Gina; Dr. Peter Rothman; and the American Countryside Farmers Market all of whom helped me in various ways.

My son, Wesley, was diagnosed at the age of nine with *eosinophilic esophagitis*, a rare allergic disorder causing internal damage to the esophagus when positive allergens are ingested. It's critical for his welfare that he avoid foods to which he's allergic. Unfortunately, his list of food allergens is lengthy and includes common ingredients like corn, dairy, peanuts, wheat, barley and rye. And that's only his short list.

Many would view this problem as troublesome and it was, but perspective in hard situations is vital. Ultimately, I realized I had two choices. I could view it as a hardship and dread each day of cooking for my young son, or I could step up and make it the biggest creative challenge of my life. I chose the latter.

Actually, before Wesley was diagnosed, I had been on several elimination diets myself because of food allergies, so all in all, I have nearly 25 years of experience using alternate ingredients. I began experimenting with lots—and I do mean lots—of different ingredients. After several months of working with recipes, I realized that I loved creating these new and different dishes. I started serving new recipes for dinner guests, took new dishes to potluck dinners and various baked goods to other social events. Most amazingly of all, I discovered that if I didn't explain to people that the food they were eating was different—allergen free—then they didn't even know it. This alone was a great compliment and became my guiding principle—to create food that leaves behind the ingredients without leaving behind the taste.

Real-People Approved, **Real-Life Tested**

Life for most families is busy and complicated enough without cooking one meal for a family member who must avoid a certain set of food allergens and another whole meal for everyone else who doesn't need to avoid anything at all. So here's the rule in my kitchen: If I cannot serve a recipe to everyone, I don't serve it to anyone. I truly offer 301 recipes so good you won't know what's missing!

The recipes in this book are real-people approved and real-life tested–most by people who have no dietary restrictions at all. My husband has zero food allergies and restrictions, and he's been my biggest fan for more than 18 years. Taste testers are not just our closest friends and family. People far and wide have tried my recipes and sampled my food and will vouch for its taste and quality.

Yet, I can tell people all about my allergy-free recipes, but until they taste the food it sounds unbelievable. Probably the best endorsement yet came one Saturday evening from a group of neighborhood children. We were expecting company for a cookout that night, and I was busy preparing the food. There were kids playing all over our yard and adjacent yards, but as busy as they were they didn't mind sampling food. Best yet, when I announced it was time for the group to head home because the food was ready for our guests, the neighborhood gang asked if they could get some "carryout"! That's an endorsement if ever I've heard one.

After many, many requests for my recipes, I published my first book in 2007, *So, What do You Eat?* It was a great beginning. However, I've been blessed with such a tremendous passion for allergy-free cooking that I couldn't stop there. How could I? There are more than 12 million people in our country who suffer from food allergies and nearly 2.3 million people who are gluten intolerant. It's true that my son lives with a more rare disorder, but the bottom line is this: It's still a food allergy challenge, and an elimination diet is still the key to his health.

Food Allergies on the **Rise**

The number of food allergy sufferers is staggering when you think about it, and the numbers continue to climb. So, I continued working on new recipes and began speaking publicly about allergy and/or elimination diets. My underlying theme has been that everyone can love allergy-free recipes because they don't have to taste like cardboard. I began teaching classes on how to cook while avoiding major ingredients like wheat, corn, dairy and peanuts. Then I took it a step further and began teaching classes on eating gluten free. Interestingly enough, our family didn't go gluten free because of Celiac disease or gluten intolerance, but because Wesley developed allergies to most grains that contain gluten. In essence, we follow the same avoidances, but for a different reason.

Almost everywhere I travel, I find someone who suffers from food allergies or who has gluten intolerance or who has a friend or family member who does. So I set out to find products that are safe for Wesley and others who must eat allergy and or gluten free. Since I search high and low, finding products isn't the big problem it used to be. However, finding products that taste great is a tougher job.

As I continued developing and compiling new recipes, *Allergy-Free Cooking Everyone Loves* was born. And it's founded on one major principle: Every single recipe must be tried and true: real-people approved and real-life

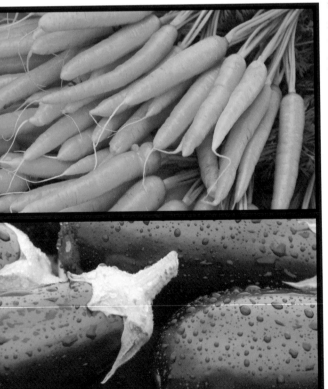

tested before it's ever considered for publication. The recipes must produce food that is appealing to the eye and maintain a texture as similar as possible to its "regular" counterpart. And plain and simple—my recipes must not just taste good—but great!

Real Family Eating with **Variety**

Keep in mind that I've created recipes of many kinds to appeal to tastes of every kind. In other words, these recipes are not "laboratory generated" with strange ingredients and an equally strange taste. They are real foods that real families like to eat—*Allergy-Free Cooking Everyone Loves*.

Since I enjoy entertaining, I've included recipes elaborate enough for dinner parties, and cookies and brownies tasty enough to be sold at school bake sales. Some of the foods are fun and tasty enough that kids don't just want to eat them, they want to get in the kitchen and cook them. Yes, moms, even kids can cook gluten or allergy free!

The only complaint I get about my food comes from my husband and son who say they rarely enjoy the same thing twice because I'm constantly trying new things. They'd like

to eat their favorites more often! That's excellent news because, again, my husband has no special dietary needs whatsoever. So even if you have no allergies, these recipes are for you too. If you're not allergic to wheat protein, you have no allergies to gluten grains or you're not gluten intolerant, simply exchange the entire amount of flour in each recipe with regular wheat flour. If you have no milk protein allergy and are not intolerant to dairy, exchange amounts of nondairy products with regular dairy products one to one. The same is true for exchanging unrefined sugars with regular sugars. But let me also encourage you to use these allergy-free recipes just to try new ingredients and eat healthier.

Quality You Can **Trust**

As you try these recipes and products I've suggested, let me assure you that any product I define by brand name is something I use in my home and in my own recipes all the time. Trust me, I'm picky. In order for me to use a product, it must meet a few criteria. It must be one of the best or the best in its category in my opinion. To help you identify product success stories that I recommend, I've created a section called *Product Resources* that begins on page 150.

Jam-Packed with **Tools**

But there's more! Since I know as well as anyone what a completely overwhelming scenario eating allergy free can create, I was determined to pack this cookbook with every helpful advantage I could offer you.

In addition to the *Product Resources*, I've included *What's What in Allergy Ingredients* to introduce and explain ingredients and their uses, *Starting a Practical Pantry* to help you get started with allergy-free basic staples, *Let's Go Shopping* to help you navigate the world of allergy-free choices and purchases, a *Crash Course in Label Reading* to guide you in deciphering ingredients and discovering hidden allergens and 301 of my very best recipes. And, finally, to make this collection the ultimate reader-friendly cookbook, I've coded each recipe with icons to help you quickly avoid your food allergens.

From my kitchen to yours, happy cooking—and welcome to allergy-free cooking you will love!

—Stephanie Hapner

The long list of alternative allergy-free ingredients can leave even the best cook wondering "what's what." Some of these terms sound like a foreign language. So here you'll find a glossary of allergy-free ingredients to make life a little easier!

Grains, Flours and **Thickeners**

Amaranth flour – Ground using an ancient grain unrelated to wheat; it can be light to very dark in color. This flour, discovered by the Aztecs, should be refrigerated or it can become very strong in flavor as it ages.

Arrowroot – A thickener like cornstarch, which begins to thicken at lower temperatures. It's a good alternative for those who need to avoid corn.

Brown rice flour – It has the same protein composition as white rice flour but adds more nutritional value. It needs to be refrigerated because it's a whole grain. Otherwise it can become rancid.

Buckwheat flour – Ground from roasted buckwheat groats, dark in color and has a strong, but rich flavor. It's many times blended with lighter flours to soften its taste.

Cassava meal – Taken from the same plant as tapioca, but stronger in flavor and not quite as light in color or texture.

Millet – Dating back to Bible days, this grain can be used in whole grain form or in flour for baking. I prefer whole cooked millet and millet cereals.

Nut meal – A finely ground mixture of tree nuts. Almond meal is the most popular, and pecan meal is second in popularity. It can be found in some commercial groceries and health food stores, or you can grind your own.

Oats – Eliminated by many gluten-intolerant people. Technically, oats are gluten free, but many gluten-sensitive people don't fair well with oats because oats are many times processed in facilities where glutinous grains also are processed. Cross contamination issues result. In the Resources section, I'm happy to list a great resource for Gluten Free Oats out of Wyoming. The company processes oats and only oats so you can be confident to use clean, certified, gluten-free oats in all your favorite foods.

Gluten-free oat flour – It has a heavier texture than some flours. I make my own by grinding Gluten Free Oats into a fine powder in my food processor. It takes about 1¼ cup of oats to make 1 cup of gluten-free oat flour. I use gluten-free oat flour for baking—not thickening because I don't prefer the consistency of the flour in sauces.

Potato starch flour – It's made from only the starch of the potato and is white. It's not to be confused with potato flour, which is made from dried, cooked and ground potatoes. I use potato starch flour in combination with other flours when baking gluten or wheat free to provide more weight and consistency to foods. I sometimes use it as a sauce thickener, but it must be combined well so that it does not form lumps.

Quinoa – Discovered by the Incas, this non-grain must be rinsed well or it has a very bitter taste because of the natural protective coating on the quinoa itself. I like to use quinoa flakes and have a Quinoa Honey cookie recipe that we really enjoy. See Brownies, Bars & Cookies, page 121.

Sorghum flour – Derived from the sorghum plant, it offers a light, mild flavor. It has become one of my favorites, and I use it in a variety of recipes.

Soy flour – This flour boosts the protein content in foods and needs to be refrigerated.

Sweet rice flour –This flour, made from "sticky" or "sushi" rice, works well when mixed with other flours. It helps give baked goods a firmer texture and helps them retain more moisture.

Tapioca flour –It originates from the cassava plant and works well mixed with other flours and in granular form as a thickener.

White rice flour – This flour is used widely for gluten-intolerant or wheat-allergic people. Unlike brown rice flour, it needs no refrigeration because the rice kernels are stripped of their nutrients and do not become rancid.

Sweeteners

Agave nectar – A liquid sweetener derived from the cactus plant and light-to-dark amber in color. Agave can be more costly than other liquid sweeteners, but it's simply sweet–like sugar–with no other distinct flavor like honey or maple syrup.

It's successfully used by many diabetics as a natural alternative to sugar because it does not elevate the glycemic index in the same way as sugar, though there have been very rare instances when agave has been problematic for a diabetic after a large meal and a large amount of food containing agave were consumed. Like all things, it should be used in moderation. It can be a great addition to a low-sugar or virtually sugar-free diet.

*Substitution: Use ¾ cup agave for each cup of sugar. Reduce the liquid in the recipe by ¼ cup. Decrease baking temperature by 25 °.

Brown sugar –Simply granulated sugar with molasses added. In fact, I use one cup sucanat with 1 teaspoon of molasses added to make brown sugar.

*Substitution: If you choose brown sugar instead of sucanat, use the same amount of packed brown sugar as the amount of sucanat in a recipe and decrease the amount of molasses by 1 teaspoon.

Dextrin, maltodextrin and dextrose – All can be derivatives of corn, but it's not always the case. Some dextrose is derived from cane sugar. Many processed deli meats and smoked meats are made with dextrose. The only way to be certain is to contact the manufacturer regarding the product.

Fructose powder –A white granular sweetener. Beware! Fructose does not necessarily mean derived from fruit. Many forms are made from corn. I don't use fructose powder because it's often sold in bulk, and it leaves too many ingredient questions unanswered.

Fruit juice concentrate – I purchase frozen fruit juice concentrate, though you must be sure you're getting 100 percent fruit juice with no added sugars. Concentrate is boiled and reduced to increase the sweetness by decreasing the volume.

Honey –The naturally sweet substance varies in color and flavor depending on the plant sources available to bees.

*Substitution: Use ¾ cup honey per 1 cup sugar and reduce liquid in the recipe by ¼ cup.

Maple sugar –Pure maple syrup boiled down into a fine, amber powder. It's great, but it's also more costly than other granular sweeteners.

Maple syrup –Sap from the maple tree that's amber to dark brown in color and available in grades ranging from a very light maple flavor to a pretty intense maple flavor.

*Substitution: Use ¾ cup of maple syrup per 1 cup of sugar and reduce the liquid in the recipe by ¼ cup.

Molasses –A byproduct of sugar cane that's rich in nutrients and dark in color with a strong flavor.

Organic sugar –Very similar to white sugar in consistency, but not bleached. When the color of a frosting is important, it's good to choose organic sugar. Turbinado sugar and sucanat will turn a "white frosting" to a maple color. Organic sugar is much lighter and looks more like its "regular" counterpart in color.

Ground organic sugar –Ground in a food processor or blender to create a finer consistency.

Powdered organic sugar – Organic sugar finely ground in a food processor or blender, then combined with potato starch flour to be used in fillings and frostings. To make powdered organic sugar, add ¼ cup potato starch flour per 1 cup finely ground organic sugar.

Stevia – Plant derived and available in liquid and powder forms. Pure stevia powder can be 250 times sweeter than sugar, though new stevia products on the market are less concentrated and more in the range of 30-40 times sweeter than sugar. If too much stevia is used, it can create a licorice aftertaste. More and more I'm experimenting with stevia in cooking and baking, but I mostly use it to sweeten fruits, coffee, tea and yogurt.

Sucanat – A dehydrated cane juice that's granular and brown. It maintains a bit of molasses flavor and is less refined than turbinado sugar. Sucanat is my granular sweetener of choice.

> *Ground sucanat* – Simply sucanat that has been processed in a food processor or blender to make it a finer consistency.

> *Powdered sucanat* – Finely ground sucanat combined with potato starch flour to be used in fillings and frostings. To make powdered sucanat, add ¼ cup potato starch flour per 1 cup of finely ground sucanat.

Turbinado sugar – Unrefined sugar with impurities removed. Actual raw sugar cannot be sold in the United States, though you'll frequently hear the term "raw sugar" describing turbinado sugar because of the renowned brand name.

> *Ground turbinado sugar* – Simply turbinado sugar ground in a food processor or blender to make it finer in consistency.

> *Powdered turbinado sugar* – Turbinado sugar finely ground in a food processor or blender and then combined with potato starch flour to be used in fillings and frostings. To make powdered turbinado sugar, add ¼ cup potato starch flour per 1 cup finely ground turbinado sugar.

Dairy **Substitutes**

Cheese substitutes (shreds • slices • chunks) – I use products made primarily from rice and soybeans. Some of them contain casein, which is milk protein. If you're intolerant to any milk protein or are unsure if you are, eliminate substitutes completely or use a vegan brand that should contain no animal products of any kind.

Cream cheese substitutes – Commonly made from rice or soy, the consistency of the substitutes are so similar to real cream cheese that the difference is undetectable in cooking and baking or when mixed with other ingredients. However, the substitute doesn't offer the same zing of tartness as regular cream cheese, so I recommend adding a splash of vinegar or lemon juice if you plan to use it as a plain spread.

Throughout the book, these products are referred to as *cream cheese substitute, rice or soy* because they're both wonderful replacements for their dairy counterpart.

Recipes calling for no other soy products are labeled as *soy free* when the rice alternative is offered.

Nondairy frozen desserts – Now offered in many commercial groceries, there are many varieties and flavors available. Some of the most popular are made from soy, rice or coconut, but be sure to check the ingredients list, especially if you choose a gourmet flavor.

Nut milk – A nondairy drink traditionally derived from tree nuts. Almond is the most popular.

Sour milk or buttermilk – Can be substituted by adding 1 tablespoon of lemon juice to 1 cup of plain soy milk and allowing it to stand for 2-3 minutes.

Soy milk – Milk made from ground soybeans available sweetened or unsweetened in several flavors and available shelf stable or refrigerated. When my recipes call for soy milk, they call for plain soy milk. If vanilla is to be used, the recipe will specify vanilla soy milk.

Soy milk powder – A powder made from dehydrated soy milk. Soy milk powder can be used to give recipes a fuller flavor, and it can be cooked with lecithin granules to make it richer for use in soups or sauces. I use Soy Quick by Ener-G Foods. See *Product Resources* for details, page 150.

Tofu – A soybean curd that can be purchased in different types and packaging. I prefer the very firm water-packed tofu for main dishes and the silken, aseptic-packaged tofu for sauces, creams and desserts.

Tofu cream cheese – Simply a soy cream cheese substitute. It is commonly called tofu cream cheese because of branding.

Tofu sour cream – Like cream cheese substitute, it's very similar to its dairy counterpart in texture and flavor. I make my own tofu sour cream, but it can also be purchased for convenience. See Master Recipes, page 20.

Vegan Parmesan – A great alternative to its dairy counterpart, it's nearly identical in flavor, though a bit more granular in texture. I use a vegan brand because it contains no casein or milk proteins. If you choose a vegetarian or dairy-free brand, it may contain casein or milk protein. Many times I mix it with cream cheese substitute, rice or soy for a spread or to make Easy Mock Ricotta. See Master Recipes, page 22.

Oils and **Fats**

Canola margarine – A soft butter substitute made primarily of canola oil that spreads easily on breads or toast. Once again, read labels carefully to find one that fits your specific dietary need.

Canola oil – An oil that's more heart-healthy than some. It has a high smoke point and can be used in cooking and baking.

Clarified butter – Butter with water, casein and whey eliminated. Clarified butter is very hard when refrigerated so it should sit out at room temperature before mixing. It can be purchased in many health food stores and is frequently marketed as ghee, a popular food item in India. See Master Recipes, page 22.

Coconut oil – Readily available, though more costly than many other oils. It solidifies at room temperature and can be used in place of other cooking oils.

Extra virgin olive oil – Simply referred to as olive oil in this publication. Extra virgin olive oil is the best grade of olive oil with the most flavor, and the best choice for salads and dressings or for dipping. It has a low-smoke point so it should not be used at extremely high temperatures as it could burn or alter flavor. It's made in many regions of the world and comes in many varieties and flavors. I enjoy using several varieties of olive oil offered by The Olive Branch. Information about specific Olive Branch products is highlighted in the *Product Resources*, page 150.

Palm shortening – Very similar to ordinary commercial shortenings. The consistency is slightly different, but it can be substituted cup for cup with its regular counterpart. Many times it's made from more than one palm resource, but because it often contains oil from the coconut palm it can be more costly.

Vinegars

Balsamic vinegar – It's prepared from grape pressings not permitted to ferment into wine. Grape pressings are boiled down to make a dark syrup and then the syrup is aged under rigid restrictions. This syrup is placed with vinegar into kegs made from oak to age. As it ages, the moisture evaporates, thickening the vinegar and concentrating the flavor. Traditional balsamic has a rich, slightly sweet flavor and brings out the sweetness of fresh fruits and berries. Because other ingredients complement the balsamic vinegar so nicely, it's now available in a wide variety of flavors. I prefer balsamic vinegars from The Olive Branch because they are superior in smoothness and flavor compared to other commercial brands I've tried in the past. See details in the *Product Resources*, page 150.

Ume plum vinegar – A byproduct of pickled umeboshi plums, which is the liquid brine left over after pickling plums. In Japan it's known as ume su, meaning plum vinegar. It's salty and tangy and colored red. It's delicious sprinkled over cooked vegetables and a great addition to many recipes.

Apple cider vinegar – A vinegar made by fermenting apple cider. The sugar in the apple cider is broken down by bacteria and yeast during the process. It turns to alcohol, then vinegar. Apple cider vinegar is a light yellow-brown color. Unfiltered and unpasteurized apple cider vinegar has dark, cloudy sediment that settles at the bottom of the bottle. Apple cider vinegar has often been praised for providing several health benefits. It contains important nutrients, including potassium, calcium and beta carotene.

White vinegar – It's made from allowing a distilled alcohol to oxidize. The clear substance is sometimes used for household cleaning. Most cooks prefer red vinegars or apple cider vinegar for cooking purposes.

Rice vinegar – This vinegar is the exception when it comes to cooking with clear vinegar because it's almost exclusively used for cooking. Rice vinegar is an important ingredient in many Asian recipes. In fact, there are two types of rice vinegar: one made from fermented white rice and the other made from sake.

Seasonings and **Flavorful Additions**

Canola mayonnaise – Mayonnaise made from only canola oil rather than another vegetable oil or a combination of oils. I usually purchase canola mayonnaise, but if you're unable to find one that fits your dietary needs, you can substitute Tofu Mayonnaise. See Sauces & Such, page 101.

Capers – They're often pickled nasturtium seeds, used in several different ways and adding a unique and pleasant addition to foods—especially vegetables, fish and poultry.

Horseradish – A root with a spicy and pungent flavor. It's minced and can be purchased in the refrigerator case. It is not the same as horseradish sauce.

Ketchup – This ever popular condiment is used in many recipes. Make sure to use a ketchup product that's acceptable for your diet. In our house we use a corn-free ketchup that contains cane juice for sweetening.

Nut butters – These spreads are very similar in appearance to peanut butter, but are made from soy beans or tree nuts—not peanuts. The nut butters listed below are all great alternatives to peanut butter. However, most are free of preservatives so it's best to refrigerate them if they won't be used in three to five weeks (depending on temperature). Otherwise, they'll become rancid. Also, most alternative nut butters are sold in natural form so the oils naturally separate, and therefore, it's a good idea to stir them thoroughly before each use.

- *Almond butter* – Made from ground almonds and comes roasted or raw.
- *Cashew butter* – Made from ground cashews and available in several varieties including crunchy, smooth, salted and unsalted.
- *Sunflower nut butter* – Made from ground sunflower seeds and available in crunchy and smooth varieties. This is one of my son's favorites!
- *Soy nut butter* – Made by grinding roasted soybeans and available in crunchy and smooth form.

Orange and lemon zest – Pieces of the outermost peel of the fruit, without the spongy, white, pith directly underneath. It can be used fresh or dried.

Salt-free blends – Simply blends of herbs and/or spices to enhance the flavor of recipes without adding salt. They can be homemade or purchased commercially.

Sea salt – It's a natural salt obtained by evaporating seawater. It's always used for cooking at my house! When one of my recipes calls for sea salt, I'm referring to an extra fine grind. Otherwise I specify coarsely-ground sea salt, which is generally too coarse to use in baked goods.

Sun-dried tomatoes – Dehydrated tomatoes, which can be purchased packaged dry or in oil. The dry-packaged tomatoes are lower in fat and can be soaked in water to hydrate for easier use.

Tamari – A premium Japanese soy sauce. While regular soy sauce contains as much as 60 percent wheat, tamari is made with primarily soybeans and only a small amount of wheat. Beware—regular tamari is NOT gluten free.

Vanilla – I always use pure vanilla, not imitation vanilla flavor. Granted, it's more expensive, but definitely superior in flavor. Also, beware, many commercial imitation vanilla extracts are *NOT* gluten free.

Wheat-free tamari – It's made with 100 percent soybeans and no wheat, therefore, it can be use in most gluten free diets.

Miscellaneous **Ingredients**

Cereals – The products our family uses are made mostly of rice and sorghum. Read labels carefully to find cereals that are free of wheat, corn and whatever else you may need to avoid in your diet.

Egg replacer – It's a blend of starches that adds leavening to baked goods. Ener-G Foods makes the best I've found; details can be found in Product Resources, page 150.

Guar gum – A fiber that aids yeast in causing baked goods to rise. Many daily fiber therapies are made primarily from guar gum.

Lecithin – A natural emulsifier, extracted primarily from soybean oil. Lecithin is an antioxidant and is present in all living cells. It can be derived from eggs and is used in cooking and baking because it's a natural water binder.

Potato chips – The product our family uses is cooked in soybean oil and lightly salted. Shop around to find a brand that fits your needs.

Textured soy protein (TSP) – A meat substitute that comes in dry crumbles and needs to be reconstituted before use. I use it in recipes instead of TVP (defined below) because it assures me that I'm using a product made only from soy with no other vegetable ingredients.

Textured vegetable protein (TVP) – Also a meat substitute, it's made from any vegetable, though it's very similar in appearance to TSP. TVP is often derived from corn, rice, peanuts and soy to name a few.

Vitamin C powder – Ascorbic acid; helps leaven baked goods.

Xanthan gum – Adds texture and helps maintain the balance of ingredients in baked goods without gluten. It helps bind the alternative flours together, giving a better consistency to the gluten-free items.

Miscellaneous **Terms**

Vegan Diet – A diet that does not include animal products of any kind—cheese, butter, eggs, etc.

Vegetarian Diet – A diet excluding all meat and fish.

Starting a **Practical Pantry**

Basic staples for the cook using gluten-free and allergy-alternative ingredients

Whether you're forced to begin an allergy-free regimen or elimination diet or you've simply decided to adopt a healthier eating lifestyle, the task can seem overwhelming. It can call for a whole new list of ingredients, which causes many to wonder, *Where and how do I begin?*

Help is here! Bringing nearly 25 years experience to the table, I've outlined below a list of key ingredients you'll need to get started. There are many alternatives on the market, but purchasing these items first will provide a good foundation for building your pantry.

And before you bring in the new, be sure to toss out the old. That's right! It's best to begin by cleaning out your pantry to eliminate items you shouldn't eat. Play detective in your cupboards and thoroughly read labels, getting rid of products not allowed on your diet regimen. If you keep them, you'll be tempted to use them. You can always give partially used food items to friends and family and unused items to a local food pantry.

Here goes!

Flours for Gluten- and **Wheat-Free Diets**

Here are four mainstays in gluten-free or grain-sensitive cooking and baking no cupboard should be without: brown rice flour, tapioca flour, white rice flour and potato starch flour. Sorghum flour is my new big favorite flour, and I often use it as a substitute for brown rice flour in recipes.

Grains for Gluten- and **Wheat-Free Diets**

Brown rice and white rice are the two most basic grains to have on hand. I also recommend adding oats to the list because they're quite versatile and can be easily ground into flour. If you're gluten sensitive, certified gluten-free oats are the choice for you. They're more costly, but safer.

For even more variety, add millet or quinoa to your pantry.

Fats for Many **Diets**

Canola oil and dairy-free canola margarine are essential. In my kitchen I also keep coconut or palm oil on hand to use in place of shortening.

Clarified butter (free of casein and whey) is another important item—especially to add more flavor in baking. Keep in mind that if you have severe symptoms from dairy, this may not be an option for you because of possible protein spill during clarification.

Milks for **Dairy-Free Diets**

Soy milk is very important to stock. I use the refrigerated variety for drinking and cereal; chocolate and vanilla with extra calcium for kids. For cooking, boxed soy milk in plain or unsweetened is fine, but shake well before using.

Rice milk is recommended for those on a soy-free diet. I prefer a brand called Rice Dream, which comes in plain, vanilla and chocolate.

Cheese Substitutes for **Dairy-Free Diets**

Nondairy Parmesan topping is another item you'll need. I use a vegan brand to ensure there's no casein (milk protein).

Cream cheese substitutes—rice or soy—are good to have in stock.

Tofu sour cream is another must have. I make it myself with silken tofu, but it can also be purchased for convenience.

Miscellaneous **Essentials**
(for many types of diets)

Here's a list of items essential to every allergen-free pantry. The list accommodates many different types of diets.

- **Baking powder** – Most baking powders contain corn, so if you're corn intolerant be sure to find a corn-free one.
- **Baking soda**
- **Cocoa** is a staple in our cupboard.
- **Dairy-free chocolate chips** – Contrary to popular belief, there's no dairy in many semi-sweet chocolate chips. **Cocoa butter** is not a dairy product; it's a fat extracted directly from the cocoa bean itself. Inspect the product label for additions of other dairy products like butter fat or milk fat.
- **Guar gum** – It can be used in place of the xanthan gum depending on your preference.
- **Pure vanilla extract** – The real deal is worth the extra expense because it offers better flavor and because some imitation vanilla contains corn and other allergens.
- **Vitamin C powder** – It can be used as a leavening agent in baked goods when other items are unsuitable.
- **Xanthan gum** – A package is pricey, about $12, but it will last a very long time because it's used in exceptionally small amounts.

Crash Course in **Label Reading**

In a perfect world, labels would be clear and to the point. For instance, corn would be corn would be corn. But, unfortunately, labels generally are not clear and to the point. In fact, to live successfully in the allergy-free world, you must become a food detective.

Here's the simple truth: Many foods that would seem safe are not. So it's important to always check labels for hidden ingredients and read labels at every purchase because manufacturers make changes in products often and without notice or warning.

The first rule of safety when reading labels is to eliminate the obvious. Any ingredient that contains the name of the allergen you must avoid is an obvious and absolute no. Another important rule of thumb is to beware of broad and obscure words. For instance, beware of these vague groupings: *natural* in natural flavorings and *vegetable* in vegetable oil. One particularly distressing catchphrase cloaked in mystery is *seasonings*. All of these words should alert you to allergen problems. Bottom line, the only one way to be certain these obscure groupings do not contain problem ingredients is to contact the food manufacturer.

Disguised **Allergens**

Listed below are some of the major allergen categories that many people need to avoid along with some of the more technical and surprising words used to identify them. Mind you, this is a "crash course" in how to read labels so I've provided only a short list of ingredients in each allergen category. It's meant as a "detective starter kit" to steer you toward the path of investigative label reading. But this is only a guide; it's not meant to replace a doctor's recommendation or an exhaustive list of food allergens your doctor may provide you. Again, if you are unsure of any ingredient, contact the food manufacturer for a complete ingredient list on a particular product.

 Corn
Baking powder
Crystalline fructose
Dextrose
Food starch
Glucose
Grits
Hominy
Maize
Maltodextrin
Modified food starch
Monosodium glutamate/MSG
Polenta
Vegetable gum
Vegetable starch

Xylitol

 Dairy
Artificial butter flavor
Casein
Caseinates
Chocolate
Hydrolysates
High protein flour
Lactalbumin
Lactoferrin
Lactoglobulin
Lactose
Lactulose
Luncheon meat, hot dogs, sausages

Margarine
Natural and artificial flavoring
Nisin
Nondairy products
Nougat
Pudding
Whey
Yogurt

Egg
Albumin
Egg substitutes
Globulin
Livetin
Macaroni and pastas

Mayonnaise
Meringue
Ovalbumin
Ovomucin
Surimi

Processed meats
Rye
Self-basting poultry
Soy based veggie burgers
Spelt
Tamari

 Wheat
Bran
Bulgar
Couscous
Cracker meal
Durum
Farina
Flour
Graham flour
Hydrolyzed vegetable protein
Matzo meals
Natural and artificial flavoring
Pasta
Semolina
Soy sauce
Starch
Vegetable gum

 Gluten
Barley
Beer
Beverage mixes
Canned broth
Caramel color
Couscous
Dry roasted nuts
Farina
Hot dogs
Kamut
Malt flavoring
Malt syrup
Meat substitutes
Modified food starch

 Soy
Edamame
Hydrolyzed soy protein
Miso
Natural and artificial flavoring
Shoyu sauce
Soya flour
Tamari
Textured vegetable protein (TVP)
Tofu
Vegetable broth
Vegetable gum
Vegetable starch

Product **Surprises**

Caution! Beware! Below are some popular food products found in the average American household, and yet, take note of some of the more common allergens each contains. I've picked examples of products that most people would consider safe choices, and beside each product is a list of allergens the product may contain. Again, the only way to be certain about specific products is to contact the manufacturer directly. Keep in mind that while one product may contain an allergen, the same product by another manufacturer may not. Remember, this is not a list of main ingredients or what the products do contain; only what *some* of these products may contain.

Artificial butter flavoring: dairy
Baked beans: corn, gluten, wheat
Baking powder: corn
Canned tomatoes and tomato sauces: corn
Cashews: peanuts
Chinese foods: corn, gluten, peanuts
Cold cuts: corn, dairy, gluten, wheat
Commercial pestos and sauces: tree nuts
Confectioner's or powdered sugar: corn
Cough syrup: corn
Dairy products: corn
Dark chocolate candy bars: corn, dairy, soy
Dried fruit mixes: corn
Dried noodles and pastas: corn, egg, gluten, wheat

Enchilada and mole sauces: gluten, peanuts
Flavored vinegars: gluten
Frozen potatoes/french fries: corn
Gluten-free baking mixes: corn
Medication tablets: corn
Nondairy whipped topping: corn, dairy
Self-basting poultry: corn, gluten
Soy cheese substitutes: dairy
Soy sauce: corn, wheat, gluten
Sunflower seeds: peanuts
Vanilla extract: corn, gluten
Vegetarian cheese substitutes: dairy, corn
Yogurt: corn

Let's Go **Shopping!**

Ideas on how and where to shop for alternative ingredients!

Shopping for alternative ingredients can be challenging if you're unfamiliar with how to look for a product or where to find it. And cost is a huge factor in eating less processed and different kinds of foods. My shopping strategies have helped us save time and pennies, and I'm passing along some ideas to help you as well.

Penny **Pinching**

First of all, most alternative products are available in cooperative markets and health food stores. Also, because gluten-free diets are becoming more necessary or more popular, many of these items are now available in commercial groceries as well. But beware! Many people assume prices will be cheaper at the commercial grocery stores, but that's not always the case. Pay attention! Health food stores and cooperative markets offer sales and flyers just like commercial groceries, and I've found better prices and better variety there.

The local health food store in my hometown also offers a monthly magazine free of charge that frequently provides coupons. It also offers a discount punch card where after you've spent a certain amount you receive a discount on your next total order. Cooperatives also frequently send out coupon books biannually to members. I've benefited from many discounts this way.

The Convenience **Factor**

Another valuable and convenient shopping tip is to purchase products online. There are several health food stores, as well as larger commercial stores and warehouses, that offer online shopping. If you check around, you can even find online stores that offer shipping deals.

Essentially I've found that shopping in more than one location is the key to saving money when working with an elimination diet. So if time and convenience are a concern, be organized and make lists. Keep track of all the staples you have on hand and the rate you go through them, and keep those lists with you at all times. We have to travel an hour to my favorite Asian market, so normally I keep a running list of items we need, and we shop there once every three months or so.

Now, let's talk food itself.

Organics: Organic food is my first choice! It offers better flavor, no chemical exposure and a lot of local product. I would like to say that we eat an all-organic diet in our house; however, I cannot. With so many limitations and the cost of food, I have to weigh the difference in cost. Much of the time, organic food is more expensive. If you want to eat more organics, I suggest you start in the produce department.

I've observed vast differences in flavor and color of fresh organic foods, so my biggest tip is to pay attention and watch for sales! At our commercial grocery, some items in the organic section are the same price as the regular items. Also, in our grocery flyer, there are now ads specifically targeting the organic and "health food" section of the store.

Cheese substitutes: Cheese substitutes can now be found in the health food section or dairy section of commercial grocery stores, and they're always available at health food stores.

Fats and oils: Most oils and unsalted butter that can be clarified are available in commercial grocery stores. Pure canola oil can sometimes be purchased at discount stores as well. I usually purchase coconut oil and canola margarines at health food stores or cooperative markets. Palm shortening is now often available in commercial grocery chains.

Flours: It's best to purchase refrigerated whole-grain flours to guarantee freshness. The best places to find refrigeration storage are cooperative markets and health food stores. Many times the flours have been packaged at these stores by hand and are available in bulk. There are also several well-known flour producers whose stock is sold in commercial groceries. Two flour brands I like are Bob's Red Mill and Ener-G Foods. I've never had a problem with rancid product. However, I always look at the expiration date stamped on the package and refrigerate or freeze the flour at home.

Another trick of the trade for me is to shop in Asian markets. They carry few whole-grain flours, so refrigeration is not an issue. But normally in the Asian markets I can find several flours at less than half the cost they are elsewhere. **Important note:** If you have any symptoms from cross contamination or are unsure if you do, be very careful shopping at Asian markets because handling procedures vary greatly from country to country.

Fruits and vegetables: Fresh is best! When fresh produce is available take advantage of it. Look through commercial grocery store flyers and mark what produce items are on sale. Design your meals around those particular items. Or, if your community has a cooperative garden or farmer's market, go there to find produce. Usually produce at a farmer's market is organically grown. So you're getting a better product for less money.

Better yet, if you have the space and a green thumb, plant and harvest your own vegetables. For several years, we've successfully grown bell peppers, tomatoes and several varieties of herbs in containers on our deck. I purchase starter plants from a greenhouse rather than planting from seed, which has worked well for me.

Grains: I normally buy my alternative grains such as millet and quinoa in a refrigerated section of my health food store. Brown rice is available in commercial grocery stores and less expensive there. I do refrigerate or freeze my whole grains at home as well. I buy other varieties of rice at an Asian market. Cross contamination is not a huge issue in our home, and the Asian market offers several kinds of rice not offered in our commercial markets.

Milks: There are a variety of milk alternatives available in commercial grocery stores now. Several larger commercial groceries are even offering their own name brands of soy milk. Milk alternatives are also available at your local health food store.

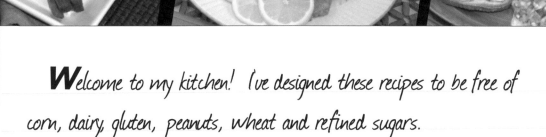

Welcome to my kitchen! I've designed these recipes to be free of corn, dairy, gluten, peanuts, wheat and refined sugars.

Sound too good to be true? Too crazy to taste fantastic? A resounding NO to both questions. Although these recipes are free of many ingredients, you'll find they taste so great you literally won't know what's missing!

I've strived to find the best ingredients and combinations out there that will be most pleasing to you and your families. Read your labels, buy your staples and get ready for a culinary journey that will bring a better quality of life to you and your family.

OK, get cooking!

       -Stephanie

Stephanie's Shorthand

You'll find these icons used throughout the book to identify which recipes are free of which allergens as well as identifying tools, special alerts and notations:

 Corn free

 Dairy free

 Egg free

 Gluten free

 Peanut free

 Soy free

 Tree nut free

 Wheat free

 Identifies info found in *What's What in Allergy Ingredients*, a glossary of what's what in allergy ingredients.

 Directs readers to *Product Resources*, where it lists products I recommend.

 The icon is used to notate a recipe when a cheese substitute is used. It may contain casein (milk protein), depending upon the brand a person chooses to use.

 This icon is used when specialty products from The Olive Branch are used. In cases where this icon is used, I strongly recommend using the exact product specified in the recipe.

 Master Recipes—or foundational recipes—referenced often throughout my recipes. These recipes are presented in a *Master Recipe* section for your convenience.

Note: Recipes calling for no other soy products are labeled as soy free when a rice or coconut alternative is offered for cream cheese substitutes or nondairy frozen desserts.

Master **Recipes**

These recipes reflect their name! They're masters—or foundational recipes—referenced often throughout the book and highlighted in recipes with an icon for your convenience.

*B*asic Baking Mix

I adapted this mix from a recipe in Gluten Free Baking by Rebecca Reilly.

> 4 cups brown rice flour
>
> 1⅓ cups potato starch flour
>
> ⅔ cup tapioca flour

Mix all flours well and store in an airtight container in the refrigerator. This mixture may be used in place of wheat flour. Makes 6 cups.

*T*ofu Sour Cream

> 1 (12-ounce) package silken tofu
>
> 3 tablespoons canola oil
>
> 3 tablespoons fresh lemon juice
>
> 1¼ teaspoons honey
>
> ½ teaspoon sea salt

In a small bowl, stir tofu until creamy. Add canola oil and lemon juice. Then slowly blend in honey and sea salt. Use this substitute for any recipe calling for sour cream. Makes 1½ cups

*S*easoned Tomato Sauce

> 3 (15-ounce) cans tomato sauce
>
> 1 tablespoon Italian seasoning
>
> 1 teaspoon basil
>
> 2 teaspoons garlic powder
>
> 1 teaspoon oregano
>
> ½ teaspoon sea salt

Pour tomato sauce into a mixing bowl. Add the remaining ingredients and stir to combine well. Freeze in 8-ounce cup portions for up to 4 weeks. Makes approximately 6 cups.

*C*hocolate Sauce

> 1 cup cocoa
>
> 1¼ cup sucanat
>
> 1 cup vanilla soy milk

In a small sauce pan, combine the cocoa and sucanat. Mix well. Place the pan over medium heat and slowly stir in the soy milk, stirring constantly. Keep stirring until the mixture just begins to bubble. Remove from heat; cool and serve. Refrigerate in an airtight container for up to 2 weeks. Makes 1 cup.

$\mathcal{E}$asy Mock Ricotta Cheese

1 cup cream cheese substitute, rice or soy
 ½ cup Tofu Sour Cream
1 egg, lightly beaten
4 tablespoons vegan Parmesan

In a medium mixing bowl blend cream cheese substitute, sour cream and beaten egg. Slowly add Parmesan; stir to combine. Makes approximately 2 cups

$\mathcal{B}$aked Tortilla Chips

6 brown rice tortillas
Sea salt

Preheat oven to 350°. Lay tortillas on baking sheet. Sprinkle sea salt evenly over tortillas. Bake for 10-15 minutes or until crispy and quite brown. If the chips stay too light, they are chewy, not crispy. Makes approximately 36 chips.

$\mathcal{C}$reamy Mashed Potatoes

4 pounds Yukon Gold potatoes, peeled and quartered
2 teaspoons sea salt, divided
 1¼ cups clarified butter, melted and divided
½ cup soy milk

Place potatoes in a stock pot and cover with water. Sprinkle with 1 teaspoon sea salt. Cook potatoes until fork tender. In a mixing bowl on low speed, blend potatoes until smooth. Add 1 cup clarified butter and mix on medium-low until all clarified butter is incorporated. Sprinkle with remaining sea salt and mix 1 minute longer. Increase speed to medium-high and add milk, scraping sides of bowl often. Whip potatoes on medium-high speed for 2-3 minutes. Pour into a serving bowl and top with remaining ¼ cup clarified butter. Serves 8-10.

$\mathcal{C}$larified Butter

If you have an extreme dairy allergy or sensitivity, clarifying butter may not be the choice for you. If not done precisely, there is the chance of whey or protein spill during the clarifying process.

1 pound unsalted butter.

Preheat oven to 250°, Place 1 pound of unsalted butter in a square baking dish and place in oven. Heat until melted and the top is foamy and crusty (about 10 minutes if the butter is room temperature). Spoon off the crusty layer and discard. Then place about 4 layers of cheesecloth in a large strainer over a 4-cup measure. Slowly pour the melted butter into the cheesecloth. Do not allow any of the whey (white milky looking part) to be poured out. After all of the golden buttery substance is in the 4-cup measure, discard the leftover white liquid. For easy measuring, I place the clarified butter by tablespoons full into ice cube trays and freeze until solid. Then I gently remove each butter cube and place into an airtight jar to keep refrigerated. Then, if I need to measure for recipes, I have tablespoon portions ready to go. Clarified butter is very hard when refrigerated, so for baking it should be room temperature before mixing.

Note: Clarified butter can be purchased in many health food stores marketed as ghee, a popular food item in India. Substitution: If clarified butter is not an appropriate option, a non-dairy or canola margarine may be substituted in recipes calling for clarified butter.

Breakfast & **Brunch**

French Toast Bake, **page 27**

Oatmeal Pancakes

2 cups gluten-free oat flour
1 cup Gluten Free Oats
2 teaspoons baking soda
1 teaspoon vitamin C powder
3 cups plus 2 tablespoons water
¼ cup canola oil
2 tablespoons maple sugar or sucanat

In a medium-sized bowl, blend together oat flour, oats, baking soda and vitamin C powder. Set aside. In another bowl mix water, canola oil and maple sugar or sucanat. Gradually blend liquid ingredients into dry ingredients, stirring until smooth. Pour by ¼ cup portions onto hot griddle. Cook until bubbly on top. Turn and cook until golden. Serve with maple syrup. Makes approximately 20 pancakes.

Buckwheat Pancakes

2 cups whole buckwheat flour
1 teaspoon baking soda
1 teaspoon vitamin C powder
½ teaspoon sea salt
1 teaspoon canola oil
1 tablespoon molasses
1 (14-ounce) can coconut milk
⅓ cup water

Heat a nonstick skillet or griddle to 375°. In a small mixing bowl combine buckwheat flour, baking soda, vitamin C powder and sea salt. Set aside. In another bowl stir together canola oil, molasses, coconut milk and water. Gradually stir liquid mixture into dry ingredients until well blended. For each pancake, pour ¼ cup of batter onto a hot griddle and cook until both sides are browned. Serve warm with maple syrup. Makes 12-18 pancakes.

Easy Pancakes

2 eggs, slightly beaten
1 cup sorghum flour
1 cup Basic Baking Mix
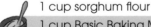
1½ cups vanilla soy milk
2 tablespoons sucanat
4 tablespoons canola oil
2 tablespoons corn-free baking powder
½ teaspoon sea salt

Heat a nonstick skillet or griddle to 375°. In a large bowl combine all ingredients and mix until smooth. For each pancake pour ¼ cup of batter onto a hot griddle. Cook pancake until bubbly on top. Turn and cook until golden brown. Makes 12-18 pancakes.

Quick & Easy Maple Oatmeal

1 cup Gluten Free Oats
½ cup water
1 tablespoon maple syrup
Soy milk (optional)

In a serving bowl, combine oats and water. Microwave on high for 1½ minutes or until water is absorbed. Add maple syrup (and soy milk if desired). Stir well; serve. Makes 2 (½ cup) servings.

Variations:

Cinna-Vanilla Oatmeal —

Add 1 teaspoon vanilla, ¼ teaspoon cinnamon and ½ tablespoon honey.

Chocolate Chip Oatmeal —

Add ¼ cup dairy-free chocolate chips.

Cinnamon Apple Raisin Oatmeal —

Add 1 tablespoon raisins, ¼ teaspoon cinnamon and 2 tablespoons unsweetened applesauce.

Millet Granola

2 cups cooked millet
1½ cups chopped pecans
2 cups raisins covered in 1 tablespoon water
2 cups unsweetened coconut
¾ cup honey

Preheat oven to 300°. In a large bowl combine cooked millet, pecans, raisins and coconut. Add honey and stir to coat. Bake for 20-30 minutes stirring every 10-15 minutes or until mixture appears dry.   Makes approximately 8 cups.

Strawberry Breakfast Shake

2 cups frozen strawberries
½ cup vanilla soy milk
½ cup orange juice

Place strawberries and vanilla soy milk in a blender. Pulse on purée until berries are smooth. Add orange juice and pulse to blend. Serve immediately. Makes 3 cups.

French Toast

3 beaten eggs
½ cup vanilla soy milk
½ teaspoon honey
½ teaspoon vanilla

6 slices Sami's Millet & Flax Bread

In a small bowl blend eggs, vanilla soy milk, honey and vanilla. Carefully dip bread slices into the mixture to fully coat both sides of the bread. Place on a griddle or skillet and cook on medium until both sides of bread are golden brown. Serve with pure maple syrup, your favorite fruit spread or fresh fruit. Makes 3 (2-slice) servings.

Breakfast Skillet

1 pound turkey sausage
½ teaspoon sage
2 tablespoons olive oil
3 medium potatoes, thinly sliced
1 small onion, chopped
½ teaspoon sea salt
8 slightly beaten eggs

In a large skillet, brown turkey sausage over medium heat. Drain sausage; sprinkle with sage and set aside. In the skillet, heat olive oil. Add potatoes and onion; cook over medium heat until potatoes begin to brown nicely. Add sea salt. Stir sausage into potatoes and onions. Pour slightly beaten eggs over mixture and cook until eggs are set. Serves 8.

Country Sausage Breakfast Casserole

6 slices Sami's Millet & Flax Bread
1 pound bulk turkey or extra lean pork sausage
¼ teaspoon ground sage
1 small onion, chopped
6 medium eggs, lightly beaten
2 cups soy milk
⅓ cup Tofu Sour Cream
½ cup vegan or soy cheddar, thinly sliced or shredded
1 teaspoon thyme

Preheat oven to 350°. Coarsely tear bread slices; set aside. In a medium skillet place the sausage, sage and chopped onion. Cook over medium heat until sausage is browned and onion is translucent. Drain excess fat; set aside. In a large mixing bowl place eggs and soy milk. Whisk together to blend; add sour cream and continue to whisk until completely combined. Add the vegan or soy cheddar slices or shreds and stir in the thyme. Place the meat mixture and the torn bread slices in a 9-by-13-inch baking dish. Pour the egg mixture over the bread and meat mixture to cover both completely. Bake for 40-45 minutes until mixture is set in the center and slightly browned. Serves 8.

French Toast Bake

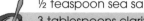

1 loaf Sami's Millet & Flax Bread, cubed
8 eggs
3 cups soy milk
2 tablespoons sucanat
1 teaspoon vanilla
½ teaspoon sea salt
3 tablespoons clarified butter
3 tablespoons sucanat
2 teaspoons cinnamon
Pure maple syrup

Place bread cubes in a buttered 9-by-13-inch baking dish. In a mixing bowl beat together the eggs, soy milk, sucanat, vanilla and sea salt. Pour egg mixture over bread. Cover and refrigerate overnight. Remove pan from refrigerator 30 minutes prior to baking. Preheat oven to 350°. Dot the top of bread mixture with clarified butter. Combine the sucanat and cinnamon; sprinkle over the top. Cover and bake for 45-50 minutes or until a knife comes out clean. Let stand 5 minutes before serving. Serve with warm maple syrup and fresh fruit. Serves 8.

Breakfast Potatoes

1 tablespoon olive oil
4 cups peeled, cubed potatoes
1 cup chopped onion
½ cup chopped celery
½ cup chopped red bell pepper
1 teaspoon minced garlic
Sea salt and Pepper

Heat olive oil in a skillet over medium heat. Stir in potatoes and cook for 3-4 minutes. Stir in the onion, celery, bell pepper and garlic. Continue to cook, stirring often until the potatoes are tender and begin to brown. Use sea salt and pepper to taste. Serves 6.

Canadian Bacon Frittata

1 teaspoon canola oil
8 eggs, well beaten
½ cup chopped onion
½ cup chopped green pepper
½ teaspoon favorite salt-free blend
¼ teaspoon garlic pepper
6 slices natural Canadian bacon
½ cup soy cheddar shreds

In a large skillet heat the canola oil. Place the eggs in a mixing bowl and stir in the onion, green pepper, salt-free blend and garlic pepper. Pour the egg mixture into the skillet; cook for 1-2 minutes. DO NOT STIR. With a spatula, carefully pull the cooked egg mixture from the edges of the skillet toward the middle, so that the uncooked egg will drain to the bottom of the skillet and begin to cook. When the middle of the egg dish has begun to set; place the Canadian bacon on top of the egg mixture. Sprinkle the top with the soy cheddar shreds and place under the broiler for 5 minutes or until the top is brown and bubbly. Cut into 6 equal wedges and serve. Serves 6.

Appetizers & **Snacks**

Shrimp Dip, **page 32**

Chili Garlic Pumpkin Seeds

½ tablespoon garlic powder

½ tablespoon basil

½ tablespoon parsley

1 teaspoon onion powder

½ tablespoon sea salt

⅓ cup canola oil

3⅓ cups pumpkin seeds

Preheat oven to 200°. Combine all of the spices in a small bowl and set aside. Pour canola oil into a small mixing bowl. Add spices and whisk until well blended. Mix pumpkin seeds with oil mixture in a larger mixing bowl and stir to coat the seeds well. Pour onto a jelly roll pan and bake for 1½ hours, stirring every 15-20 minutes. When finished, pour onto a folded newspaper layered with paper towels to cool and dry. Makes 3 ⅓ cups.

Chili Cheese Dip

2 (15-ounce) cans turkey chili with beans

1 (14-ounce) can diced, fire-roasted tomatoes

⅓ cup green chilies, chopped

1 (15-ounce) can black beans, rinsed and drained

 ⅓ cup Tofu Sour Cream

1 teaspoon sea salt

½ teaspoon cumin

½ tablespoon chili powder

1¼ cups soy cheddar shreds, divided

3-4 scallions, chopped

In a medium saucepan, heat turkey chili, tomatoes, green chilies and black beans on medium heat until heated through. Add sour cream and spices; stir to mix. Blend in 1 cup of the soy cheddar shreds and stir until melted. Pour into a serving bowl and top with remaining ¼ cup soy cheddar shreds and scallions; serve immediately. Serves 15-20.

Snack Tip! Freeze grapes for a nutritious and delicious quick snack for kids—and adults too!

Fresh Tomato Salsa

    1 tablespoon minced garlic

    2 large onions, chopped

    1 pound tomatoes, peeled, seeded and chopped

    1 teaspoon fresh cilantro, chopped, stems removed

    2 fresh jalapeno peppers

    Juice of 1 lemon

In a mixing bowl combine garlic, onions, tomatoes and cilantro and set aside. Wearing rubber gloves, cut jalapenos in half lengthwise and discard the core. With a small paring knife, scrape out the seeds and cut away the fleshy white ribs along the peppers. Cut peppers into long strips and then into a fine dice. Add diced peppers to the tomato mixture and stir well. Add lemon juice and stir to combine. Let stand at least 30 minutes before serving. Makes approximately 4 cups.

Guacamole

    2 ripe avocados, peeled and mashed (reserve one pit and set aside)

    1 teaspoon minced garlic

    3 scallions, chopped

    1 small tomato, seeded and chopped

    1 teaspoon dried cilantro leaves or 1 tablespoon fresh (stems removed)

    ¼ fresh lemon, juiced

    ½ teaspoon sea salt

    ¼ teaspoon black pepper

In a small bowl, combine avocados, garlic, scallions and tomato. Stir to combine; add cilantro, lemon juice, sea salt and pepper. Mix well and serve immediately, placing the pit appealingly in the middle of the dish so the guacamole will not discolor. Makes approximately 2 cups.

Quick & Easy Bread Pizzas

    4 slices Sami's Millet & Flax Bread

    6 tablespoons Greek Olive Spread (recipe follows)

    4 thin slices fresh tomato

    4 teaspoons vegan Parmesan

Preheat oven to 400°. Spread each slice of bread with 1½ tablespoons of olive spread. Place a fresh tomato slice and one teaspoon vegan Parmesan on top of the spread. Bake bread slices for 5 minutes. Cut each slice into four pieces for an appetizer course or serve with a green salad for a light lunch. Makes 8 appetizers or 4 lunches.

Greek Olive Spread

    1 (6-ounce) jar pitted mixed Greek or kalamata olives drained; with 1/8 cup of the liquid reserved

    1½ tablespoon capers, drained

    1 tablespoon minced garlic

In a food processor bowl, blend olives, capers and garlic together until well blended. Add the liquid from the olives and blend until it is spreading consistency. Makes approximately 1 cup.

Honey Roasted Cashews

    3 cups raw cashews
    2 tablespoons canola oil
    ½ cup honey
    ½ teaspoon cinnamon
    ½ teaspoon grated orange peel

Combine all ingredients in a microwave-safe bowl. Stir well to mix. Cook on high for 5-7 minutes, stirring halfway through cooking time. Spread nut mixture on a foil-covered baking sheet until cooled and dry. Store in an airtight container and do not refrigerate or the nuts will become sticky. Makes 3 cups.

Broiled Grapefruit Halves

    2 red grapefruits, room temperature and cut in half
    ½ cup maple syrup
    1 teaspoon canola oil
    ½ teaspoon nutmeg
    2 teaspoons cinnamon

Preheat oven to broil (500°). After halving the grapefruits, cut around each segment of the grapefruit with a sharp knife for easier eating. Place the fruit halves on a foil-covered baking sheet or broiler pan. In a small bowl combine maple syrup, canola oil, nutmeg and cinnamon. Spoon the mixture evenly over each grapefruit half and place under the broiler for 5-7 minutes or until golden on top. Serves 4.

Crabmeat Party Dip

    ½ cup Tofu Sour Cream
    1 (3-ounce) package cream cheese substitute, rice or soy at room temperature
    1 tablespoon fresh lemon juice
    1 tablespoon shredded horseradish (not horseradish sauce)
    1 tablespoon chopped pimentos
    Pinch of cayenne pepper
    ¾ cup chunked crabmeat

In a small mixing bowl combine sour cream, cream cheese substitute, lemon juice, horseradish, pimentos and cayenne. Fold crabmeat into the mixture until combined. Place in a small heated crock and serve with crackers or bread. Serves 8.

Shrimp Dip

The original Shrimp Dip recipe was given to my mother years ago by a friend. It has been tradition for our family to have this dip during the Christmas and New Year's holidays. I adjusted the ingredients to make it as true to the original as possible.

- 1 (12-ounce) package cooked shrimp, thawed and tails removed
- 1 (8-ounce) package cream cheese substitute, rice or soy at room temperature
- 1 cup ketchup
- 2 teaspoons chili powder
- 1 tablespoon chopped onion
- 2 tablespoons minced horseradish

Rinse shrimp, place in a bowl and set aside. In a small bowl combine cream cheese substitute, ketchup, chili powder, onion and horseradish. Fold shrimp into mixture, chill and serve with chips or crackers. Makes approximately 4 cups.

Spicy Salsa

- 2 large tomatoes, peeled, seeded and chopped
- ⅓ cup chopped onion
- 3 tablespoons chopped green chilies
- ⅛ teaspoon hot chili garlic sauce
- 1½ tablespoons balsamic vinegar
- 1 tablespoon freshly chopped parsley
- ½ tablespoon freshly chopped basil
- ¼ teaspoon cumin

In a small mixing bowl combine tomatoes, onion and green chilies. Stir in chili garlic sauce and balsamic vinegar. Add parsley, basil and cumin; stir to combine. Refrigerate for one hour before serving. Makes approximately 3 cups.

Snack Tip! Create an Indian summer refresher by freezing apple cider in ice cube trays; then serve the kids an icy, tasty treat.

Crab & Mushroom Appetizers

1 pound fresh button mushrooms
6 tablespoons clarified butter, divided
⅓ cup chopped onion
4 tablespoons minced roasted red bell pepper
4 ounces crab meat, flaked
1 cup fresh Millet & Flax Bread bread crumbs
1 teaspoon garlic powder
⅛ teaspoon sea salt
⅛ teaspoon garlic pepper
¼ cup vegan Parmesan

Preheat oven to 350°. Clean and trim mushrooms. Remove remaining stems; chop and set aside. Melt 2 tablespoons of clarified butter; brush over tops of mushroom caps. In a shallow buttered baking dish, place mushroom caps in one even layer. Melt remaining clarified butter in skillet over medium heat. Add chopped mushroom stems, chopped onion and roasted red bell pepper. Cook until vegetables are tender. Combine vegetables with the crab meat, fresh bread crumbs, seasonings and vegan Parmesan. Fill each mushroom cap generously with stuffing mixture. Bake for 15-20 minutes or until the mushroom caps are tender and the stuffing is lightly browned. Makes approximately 15-18 appetizers.

Spicy Tortilla Chips

1 package brown rice tortillas
¼ teaspoon paprika
1 tablespoon parsley
1 teaspoon garlic sea salt
½ teaspoon garlic pepper

Preheat oven to 400°. On two baking sheets, place tortillas in a single layer. Cut some of the tortillas to make them fit so they do not overlap. Set aside. In a small bowl combine paprika, parsley, garlic sea salt and garlic pepper. Stir to blend. Sprinkle the tortillas generously with the mixture. Bake for 15 minutes or until dark golden brown. Repeat the process until all tortillas are baked. Makes approximately 48 chips.

Raspberry Fruit Dip

½ cup Tofu Sour Cream
2 tablespoons Red Raspberry Freezer Jam (See Sauces & Such, page 104) or 100% raspberry fruit spread
¼ teaspoon vanilla

In a small bowl stir together the sour cream, jam or fruit spread and the vanilla. Combine well. Serve with fresh fruit slices. Makes approximately ½ cup.

No Peanut Peanut Butter Dip

 4 ounces Tofu Sour Cream

⅓ cup soy nut butter

1½ tablespoons honey

In a small mixing bowl combine the sour cream, soy nut butter and honey. Blend until smooth. Serve with assorted fresh fruit. Makes approximately 1 cup.

Cheesy Crabmeat Dip

 8 ounces cream cheese substitute, rice or soy at room temperature

1 tablespoon clarified butter, softened

1 tablespoon freshly squeezed lemon juice

2 tablespoons garlic powder

2 tablespoons vegan Parmesan

1 cup chunked crab meat

Preheat oven to 350°. In a small mixing bowl cream together the cream cheese substitute and clarified butter. Stir in the lemon juice, garlic powder and vegan Parmesan. Blend well. Fold in the crab meat. Spread evenly into a 9-inch pie plate and bake for 15 minutes or until hot and bubbly. Serve with Crispy Lavash Crackers, or Bread Stick Crudite. See Breads, Muffins & Crackers, pages 45 & 46. Makes approximately 1½ cups.

Bacon-Wrapped Figs

20 kalamata string figs

20 natural turkey bacon strips

½ cup balsamic vinegar

Wrap each fig with a strip of turkey bacon and hold in place with a wooden toothpick. Place the bacon-wrapped figs in a large skillet over medium heat and cook on one side until browned. Turn each fig to cook other side and stir in balsamic vinegar. Continue cooking, gently stirring often until the bacon is cooked through and the balsamic vinegar has reduced and thickened. Serve each fig with a small amount of balsamic glaze (from the pan). Makes 20 appetizers.

Fresh Tomato Bruschetta

½ cup diced tomatoes

1 tablespoon minced onion

½ teaspoon freshly chopped basil

½ teaspoon freshly chopped oregano

½ teaspoon sherry wine vinegar

⅛ teaspoon sea salt

6-8 pieces thinly sliced Sara's French Bread (See Breads, Muffins & Crackers, page 42)

In a small bowl combine tomatoes, onion, basil and oregano. Mix well. Stir in the sherry wine vinegar and sea salt and combine. Place a generous amount of tomato mixture on each slice of Sara's French Bread. Serves 6-8.

Spinach & Artichoke Bruschetta

½ cup drained, chopped marinated artichoke hearts

½ cup vegan Parmesan

2 tablespoons minced onion

2 tablespoons minced garlic

3 tablespoons canola mayonnaise

2 tablespoons Artichoke Aioli (See Sauces & Such, page 105)

½ cup chopped, fresh spinach leaves

12-14 pieces Sara's French Bread (See Breads, Muffins & Crackers, page 42) thinly sliced

Preheat oven to broil, 450°. In a chopper or food processor combine the artichoke hearts, vegan Parmesan, onion, garlic, canola mayonnaise and Artichoke Aioli. Pulse several times until mixture is smooth. Pour mixture into a small bowl and fold in spinach leaves until well blended. Place by generous tablespoonfuls atop each slice of Sara's French Bread. Broil for 4-5 minutes until tops are golden and bread is slightly crisp. Makes 12-14 appetizers.

Fried Onions

Canola oil

2 large yellow onions, very thinly sliced and separated into rings

⅓ cup sorghum flour

Sea salt

Preheat canola oil in deep fryer to 300°. Place onion rings in a large mixing bowl, sprinkle with sorghum flour and toss to coat onions. Shake excess flour from onion rings and fry for 5-7 minutes or until golden brown and crisp. It's recommended to fry in 5 or 6 small batches. Remove from fryer and drain on double layers of paper towels. Sprinkle with sea salt. Makes 8-10 snack-size portions.

Beverages

Strawberry Breakfast Shake, **page 25**

Berry Yogurt Smoothie

    4 ounces plain soy yogurt
    2 cups berries of choice
    1 tablespoon honey
    12 ice cubes

Pour yogurt, berries and honey into a blender. Blend on medium until the ingredients are well combined. Add ice cubes 3 or 4 at a time and pulse on ice crush until the cubes are crushed and mixed. Serve immediately. Makes 3 cups.

Pineapple Iced Tea

    ½ gallon unsweetened tea, freshly brewed
    4 cups unsweetened pineapple juice
    Fresh pineapple slices or pineapple slices in 100% juice

Place the tea into a gallon container. Slowly add the pineapple juice and stir well. Serve over ice with ½ slice of pineapple. Makes 12 (8-ounce) servings.

Just Peachy Banana Smoothie

    2 large peaches pitted and chunked
    1 medium banana, peeled and chunked
    1 tablespoon 100% peach fruit spread
    ¼ cup vanilla soy milk
    6 ice cubes

Place peaches, banana and fruit spread in a blender. Pulse until the fruit is blended smoothly. Add the vanilla soy milk and pulse until mixed. Add the ice 3 cubes at a time, pulsing until cubes are crushed and mixed. Serve immediately. Serves 2.

Hot & Spicy Cider

    ½ gallon apple cider
    1 broken cinnamon stick
    3 whole cloves
    2 orange slices, seeded

In a medium saucepan combine the cider, cinnamon stick, cloves and orange slices. Bring the mixture to a boil and cook for 2-3 minutes. Remove from heat; remove the cinnamon, cloves and orange slices. Pour cider into a crock pot set on warm and serve. Serves 8.

Sparkling Cranberry Punch

    1 quart 100% cranberry juice
    2 cups 100% white grape juice
    1 liter sparkling water
    1 medium lime

In a gallon pitcher, mix cranberry juice and white grape juice. Pour sparkling water into the pitcher and stir lightly. Cut lime into thin wedges. Serve over ice with a lime twist. Serves 10-12.

Mock Mimosas

    4 cups not-from-concentrate orange juice, chilled, divided
    2 cups club soda, chilled, divided
    4 orange slices for garnish

Into 4 tall glasses, pour one cup of orange juice and ½ cup of club soda. Add an orange slice to the side of the glass for garnish and serve. Serves 4.

Chocolate-Covered Banana Shake

    2 medium bananas, peeled and chunked
    4-5 scoops frozen chocolate nondairy dessert
    1½ cups chocolate soy milk

Put banana chunks into a blender and pulse on purée. Add frozen dessert and pulse on purée until mixed well. Add chocolate soy milk and blend until combined. Serve immediately. Serves 4.

Ginger Vanilla Chai

    4 cups water
    1 tablespoon cinnamon
    8 whole cloves
    ½ tablespoon cardamom
    ½ teaspoon freshly grated nutmeg
    ¼ cup fresh ginger root, cut into thin strips
    2 family size teabags
    3 tablespoons sucanat
    2 teaspoons vanilla
    ½ cup honey
    4 cups soy milk

In a 3-quart sauce pan, heat the water on medium. Combine cinnamon, cloves, cardamom and nutmeg and place them in a 6-by-6-inch piece of folded cheese cloth and tie. When the water begins to boil, add the cheese cloth bag with the spices, ginger root, teabags, sucanat, vanilla and honey. Steep for 6 minutes, then remove from heat. Remove the cheese cloth bag with the spices and the teabags and discard. Strain the ginger root from the tea. Place the tea in a ½ gallon pitcher and stir in the soy milk. Serve hot or chilled. Serves 8.

Hot Buttered Apple Drink

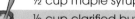

- 32 ounces 100% apple juice
- ½ cup maple syrup
- ½ cup clarified butter, softened
- ¼ cup sucanat
- 1 teaspoon freshly ground nutmeg
- ¼ teaspoon allspice
- ½ teaspoon cinnamon

In a large stockpot, pour the apple juice and the maple syrup. Cover and cook on medium, stirring occasionally. In a small saucepan, place the softened clarified butter, sucanat, nutmeg, allspice and cinnamon. Stir constantly over medium heat until the sucanat is completely dissolved. Pour hot juice mixture into single mugs and top with a tablespoon of the buttered mixture immediately before serving. If serving a crowd, the buttered mixture may be poured into the juice, poured into cups and served immediately. Makes approximately 10 (4-ounce) servings.

Smoothie Tip!

If you have smoothie lovers in your household, keep frozen berries on hand to add the number specified to your favorite smoothie recipes. Berries are easier to slice evenly while partially frozen.

Breads, Muffins & **Crackers**

$\mathcal{A}$maranth Tortillas

2¼ cups amaranth flour
¾ teaspoon sea salt
¾ cup water

Stir together flour and sea salt. Add water and stir until mixed. Then, knead to form stiff dough. Divide into 4 portions for large tortillas or 6 portions for small. Flour each portion and roll it out to ⅛ inch or less on a well-floured surface, using 2 tablespoons of flour on board. Place tortillas on a griddle and cook on both sides until lightly browned. Serves 4-6.

$\mathcal{O}$at Biscuits

1¾ cups gluten-free oat flour
¼ cup Gluten Free Oats
1½ teaspoons corn-free baking powder
½ teaspoon sea salt
¼ cup canola oil
½ cup water

Preheat oven to 400°. Stir oat flour, oats, corn-free baking powder and sea salt together in a medium bowl. Blend in canola oil with a fork until the mixture crumbles. Stir in water and pat dough on a floured board with fingers to a ½-inch thickness. Cut dough with biscuit cutter and bake on a buttered cookie sheet for 20 minutes. Makes approximately 12 biscuits.

$\mathcal{S}$ara's French Bread & Rice Pizza Crust Dry Mix

½ cup sweet rice flour
6½ cups white rice flour
5 cups tapioca flour
4 tablespoons xanthan gum
4 tablespoons plain gelatin
¼ cup Egg Replacer
½ cup sucanat

Mix all ingredients well and store in an airtight container at room temperature.
Makes approximately 14 cups.

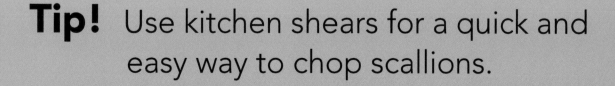

Tip! Use kitchen shears for a quick and easy way to chop scallions.

$\mathcal{S}$ara's French Bread

My friend Sara, who is allergic to wheat, shared this recipe with me. I modified it to fit our diet and I keep a large container of dry mix ready so I can prepare the bread or make a pizza anytime.

> 3½ cups prepared Sara's French Bread and Rice Pizza Crust Dry Mix (See Breads, Muffins & Crackers, page 41)
>
> 6 tablespoons soy milk powder
>
> 1 teaspoon sea salt
>
> 1 teaspoon corn-free baking powder
>
> 1 tablespoon quick-rise yeast
>
> 2 eggs
>
> 1 teaspoon apple cider vinegar
>
> 3 tablespoons canola oil
>
> 1⅓ cups warm water, divided (115-120°)

Preheat oven to 425°. In a heavy mixing bowl combine prepared dry mix, soy milk powder, sea salt, corn-free baking powder and yeast. Set aside. In a small bowl beat eggs, apple cider vinegar and canola oil with a fork to combine. Add 1 cup of the warm water and stir. Add wet ingredients to the dry mixture and beat on high for 2-3 minutes. Check after a minute to see if additional water is needed. The dough will be thick and sticky. Place oil on hands and top of dough. Form ½ of dough into a French loaf and place on a buttered cookie sheet. Repeat with the second ½ of dough. Cover loaves with a damp linen towel and let rise for 35 minutes. Bake for 60-75 minutes or until the top of the loaf is golden brown. Makes 2 small loaves.

$\mathcal{R}$ice Pizza Crust

> 3 cups prepared Sara's French Bread and Rice Pizza Crust Dry Mix (See Breads, Muffins & Crackers, page 41)
>
> ⅓ cup soy milk powder
>
> 1 teaspoon sea salt
>
> 1 tablespoon quick-rise yeast
>
> 2 eggs
>
> 1 teaspoon apple cider vinegar
>
> ½ cup warm water (115-120°), divided

Preheat oven to 400° and butter two cookie sheets or pizza pans. Blend together prepared dry mix, soy milk powder, sea salt and quick-rise yeast. Set aside. In a mixing bowl combine eggs, apple cider vinegar and 1 cup of water. Blend liquid ingredients on low for 30 seconds. Slowly incorporate the dry mixture and beat on high for 3 minutes, adding the remaining water if the mixture is too dry. Divide dough evenly on 2 pans and spread into circles leaving about a ¼-inch of an edge around. Cover and let rise in a warm place for 10 to 15 minutes and then pre-bake the crusts for 10 minutes. Remove from oven, top with sauce and favorite toppings then bake for 20–25 minutes longer. Makes 2 pizza crusts. These freeze well.

Tip! Keep a grocery list on the refrigerator. When the last of an item is used, it can be added to the list.

$\mathcal{S}$orghum Flour Bread

1 cup sorghum flour

½ cup tapioca flour

½ teaspoon sea salt

½ cup arrowroot

1½ teaspoons xanthan gum

⅓ cup soy milk powder

½ teaspoon plain gelatin

1 teaspoon Egg Replacer

2 tablespoons sucanat

1 package quick-rise yeast

2 eggs

2½ tablespoons clarified butter

½ teaspoon apple cider vinegar

1¼ cups warm water (115-120°), divided

Preheat oven to 400°. Butter, then dust loaf pan with sorghum flour. Combine sorghum and tapioca flours, sea salt, arrowroot, xanthan gum, soy milk powder, gelatin, Egg Replacer, sucanat and yeast in a large bowl and set aside. In a heavy mixing bowl whisk the eggs with a fork; add clarified butter, apple cider vinegar and 1 cup of water. Begin mixing on low speed and add dry ingredients slowly. After blending slightly, add remaining ¼ cup water if dough seems to be too dry. Beat dough on high for 3-4 minutes. Put in prepared loaf pan, cover with a wet linen towel, and let rise in a warm place for about 40-45 minutes. Bake for 50-60 minutes, covering with foil for the first 8-10 minutes of baking to prevent too much browning. Makes 1 loaf.

$\mathcal{B}$anana Muffins

1½ cups Basic Baking Mix

1 tablespoon molasses

¾ cup sucanat

1 tablespoon corn-free baking powder

1 teaspoon cinnamon

½ teaspoon xanthan gum

⅛ teaspoon sea salt

2 very ripe bananas, peeled and mashed

½ cup vanilla soy milk

⅓ cup canola oil

1 egg

1 teaspoon lemon juice

Cinnamon and sucanat or Streusel Topping, for sprinkling (See Desserts, page 116)

Preheat the oven to 350°. Line 12 muffin cups with paper liners. Mix together baking mix, molasses, sucanat, corn-free baking powder, cinnamon, xanthan gum and sea salt in a small mixing bowl and set aside. In another bowl, lightly stir together the bananas, vanilla soy milk, canola oil, egg and lemon juice until blended. Pour the liquid mixture into the dry mixture; stir until well blended. Pour batter into muffin cups and fill about ⅔ full. Sprinkle with sucanat and sugar or streusel topping and bake for 18-20 minutes or until golden brown. Makes 12 muffins.

Sweet Oat Muffins

1½ cups gluten-free oat flour
½ cup Gluten Free Oats
¼ teaspoon sea salt
1 teaspoon baking soda
¼ teaspoon vitamin C powder
⅛ cup canola oil
⅛ cup unsweetened applesauce
½ cup honey
½ cup water

Preheat oven to 400°. In a medium mixing bowl, combine oat flour, oats, sea salt, baking soda and vitamin C powder; set aside. In another bowl combine canola oil, applesauce, honey and water. Add wet mixture into dry ingredients while stirring. Pour into paper-lined muffin tins, filling about ¾ full. Bake for 15-20 minutes or until golden brown. Makes 12 muffins.

Quinoa Applesauce Muffins

¼ cup sweet rice flour
¼ cup brown rice flour
½ cup quinoa flakes
2 teaspoons corn-free baking powder
1 teaspoon baking soda
½ teaspoon sea salt
2 eggs, slightly beaten
¼ cup honey
1 cup unsweetened applesauce

Preheat oven to 400°. In a large mixing bowl combine the flours, quinoa flakes, corn-free baking powder, baking soda, and sea salt. Set aside. In a small mixing bowl combine the eggs, honey and applesauce and stir to combine. Add liquid ingredients to dry ingredients and stir until combined well. Spoon the mixture into paper-lined muffin cups, filling about ¾ full. Bake for 18-20 minutes. Makes 12 muffins.

Herbed Cassava Crackers

2 cups cassava meal
½ teaspoon baking soda
¼ teaspoon vitamin C powder
½ teaspoon sea salt
1 teaspoon favorite salt-free blend
¼ teaspoon garlic powder
½ teaspoon parsley flakes
¾ cup water
¼ cup canola oil
Coarse sea salt

Preheat oven to 325°. Mix cassava meal, baking soda, vitamin C powder, sea salt and herbs together in a large mixing bowl. Combine water and canola oil and stir into the dry mixture. Roll and/or press the dough firmly into a 12-by-15-inch pan. The dough should be ⅛-inch thick when pressed. Cut dough into 1- or 1½-inch squares. Sprinkle with coarse sea salt and bake for 30-33 minutes or until crisp. Makes 120-180 crackers.

 apioca Chips

These are great to use in place of tortilla chips.

- 1 cup tapioca flour
- ¼ teaspoon baking soda
- ½ teaspoon sea salt
- ⅛ teaspoon vitamin C powder
- 7-8 tablespoons coconut milk

Preheat oven to 350°. In a small bowl, mix together tapioca flour, baking soda, sea salt and vitamin C powder. Add coconut milk 1 tablespoon at a time; forming a stiff dough. Drop by teaspoonfuls on a parchment-lined baking sheet and flatten into thin chip forms less than ⅛-inch thick. Bake for 10-15 minutes or until edges start to brown. Makes 2-3 dozen chips.

✐ arlic Parmesan Biscuits

- 1 (12.3-ounce) package silken tofu
- 1¾ cup Basic Baking Mix
- ¼ cup sweet rice flour
- 4 teaspoons corn-free baking powder
- ½ teaspoon sea salt
- 2 tablespoons vegan Parmesan

- ¼ teaspoon garlic powder
- 4 tablespoons clarified butter, softened
- ¼ cup soy milk

Preheat oven to 375°. In a small mixing bowl stir the silken tofu until it becomes creamy; set aside. In another mixing bowl, sift together the baking mix, sweet rice flour, baking powder, sea salt, vegan Parmesan and garlic powder. Cut the softened butter into the dry mixture with a pastry blender until the mixture is crumbly. Stir in the creamed tofu and blend the dough. Add the soy milk until the mixture forms a sticky dough. Drop in even dollops on a buttered baking sheet and bake for 12-15 minutes or until golden on top. Makes approximately 12-15 biscuits.

✐ rispy Lavash Crackers

- 4 pieces Sami's Millet Lavash
- Sea salt

Preheat oven to 350°. Cut lavash bread into ¾-inch strips and place on a baking sheet and sprinkle with sea salt. Place in oven and bake for 8-10 minutes or until golden. Cool and serve with soup or appetizers. Makes approximately 20 pieces.

*B*readstick Crudite

3 slices Sami's Millet & Flax Bread
3 teaspoons clarified butter
½ teaspoon parsley

Preheat oven to 350°. Spread one teaspoon of the clarified butter onto each slice of bread. Cut each slice into four even strips and sprinkle the bread sticks with parsley. Bake for 12-14 minutes until slightly crunchy. Makes 12 breadsticks.

*P*armesan Toast Strips

4 slices Sami's Millet & Flax Bread
¼ cup melted clarified butter
½ teaspoon garlic salt
¼ cup vegan Parmesan

Preheat oven to 400°. Cut each piece of bread into 5 strips. Combine clarified butter and garlic salt. Roll bread strips into butter mixture, completely coating all sides. Sprinkle top side of each strip with vegan Parmesan; place on baking sheet. Bake 5-7 minutes until crispy. Makes 20 toast strips.

Main **Dishes**

Vegetable Mai Fun, **page 54**

$\mathcal{T}$urkey Eggplant Parmesan

    1 tablespoon olive oil
    6 turkey breast fillets
    2 tablespoons chopped garlic
    2 teaspoons basil
    1 teaspoon oregano

In a skillet, heat olive oil over medium heat. Add turkey fillets and garlic. Sauté meat and garlic until turkey is beginning to brown on one side. Turn fillets and add basil and oregano. Continue to cook until second side is browned.

Sauce:

    1 tablespoon olive oil
    ½ cup finely chopped onion
    1½ teaspoons fennel seed
    3 teaspoons sea salt
    1 small can (2¼-ounce) sliced black olives
    1 (28-ounce) can diced tomatoes
    2 (15-ounce) cans tomato sauce
    ½ teaspoon Italian seasoning
    2 medium eggplants, peeled and cut into ¼- inch slices
    ¾ cup vegan Parmesan, divided

Preheat oven to 350°. In a large saucepan, heat olive oil. Add onion and cook over medium heat until translucent. Add fennel seed; cook 2-3 minutes to toast seeds. Add sea salt, olives, tomatoes, tomato sauce and Italian seasoning. Bring to a boil, stirring occasionally. Remove from heat and set aside. Generously butter a deep 10-by-13-inch baking pan. Place a layer of sliced eggplant and top with ⅓ of sauce. Place turkey fillets on top of sauce. Then sprinkle with ¼ cup of the Parmesan. Add remaining eggplant; cover with last portion of sauce and sprinkle with remaining Parmesan. Bake for 60-75 minutes until the top is golden brown. Serves 6.

$\mathcal{S}$hepherd's Pie

    ½ cup crushed rice crackers
    1 pound ground turkey
    3 tablespoons minced onion
    1 tablespoon mustard
    ¼ cup ketchup
    1 egg, beaten
    1 bag frozen French cut green beans (thawed)
 3 cups Creamy Mashed Potatoes
    1 cup soy cheddar shreds

Preheat oven 375°. In a medium bowl mix crackers, ground turkey, onion, mustard, ketchup, and egg together until well blended. Place mixture in an 8-by-8-inch square pan and pat into a 1-inch layer. Pour green beans over meat layer and top with prepared mashed potatoes. Bake for 30 minutes. Remove from oven, sprinkle top with soy cheddar shreds and bake an additional 5 minutes until cheese is bubbly. Serves 6-8.

Spinach Loaf

3 cups dried Sami's Millet & Flax Bread, cubed

4 eggs slightly beaten

½ cup diced white onion

1 box frozen spinach thawed, drained and squeezed dry

¾ cup soy cheddar shreds

1 teaspoon ground sage

1 teaspoon thyme

1 teaspoon garlic powder

1 teaspoon sea salt

Preheat oven to 350°. Place dried bread in a large mixing bowl and set aside. In another bowl, place beaten eggs, onion, spinach and soy cheddar shreds and combine well. Add sage, thyme, garlic powder and sea salt and stir again. Pour egg mixture over bread cubes and stir to coat well. Place in a buttered loaf pan and bake for 60 minutes or until top is golden brown. Serves 6.

Traditional Lasagna

1 pound ground beef

1 onion, chopped

½ cup mixed bell peppers, chopped

4 cups tomato sauce

2 teaspoons Italian seasoning

½ teaspoon oregano

¾ teaspoon black pepper, divided

½ teaspoon sea salt

1 cup cream cheese substitute, rice or soy at room temperature

1¼ cup Tofu Sour Cream

¾ cup vegan Parmesan

1 egg, well beaten

Rice lasagna noodles, uncooked

In a large skillet, over medium heat, brown ground beef; drain. Add the onion and bell peppers. Cook until the vegetables become tender. Add the tomato sauce, Italian seasoning, oregano, ½ teaspoon of the black pepper and the sea salt. Mix well; set aside. In a small bowl combine the cream cheese substitute, sour cream, vegan Parmesan, the remaining black pepper and the egg. Pour ½ of the meat mixture into a 9-by-13-inch buttered baking dish. Place one layer of uncooked lasagna noodles on top of the meat and then place ½ of the cheese mixture atop the noodles. Repeat the process, cover and bake for 1 hour or until the noodles are tender. Serves 8.

Tip! When cooking rice noodles or rice make an extra batch. Refrigerate leftovers and use in stir-fries and casseroles. Wallah!

Ground Beef Fajitas

 1 pound ground beef
 1 teaspoon cumin
 1 tablespoon chopped garlic
 2 onions, sliced lengthwise
 2 large bell peppers, seeded and sliced
 Brown rice tortillas or Baked Tortilla Chips

In a large skillet, brown the ground beef over medium heat. Stir in cumin and chopped garlic; add onion and bell pepper slices. Cook covered for 13-15 minutes, stirring occasionally. Uncover and cook for 2-3 minutes longer until the vegetables are tender. Serve mixture rolled in warm brown rice tortillas or serve with tortilla chips. Serves 4.

Layered Chicken Fajitas

 2 tablespoons crushed garlic
 2 medium onions, sliced thinly
 2 green bell peppers, sliced thinly
 1 red bell pepper, sliced thinly
 2 (10 ounce) cans chunk chicken
 4 brown rice tortillas
 1 cup soy cheddar shreds

Preheat oven to 350°. In a skillet sauté the garlic, onions, green and red bell peppers. Cook on medium until crisp tender. Set aside. In a 9-by-13-inch buttered baking dish layer 2 of the tortillas, spoon ½ of the sautéed vegetables on top, then scatter ½ of the chicken on top of the vegetables. Repeat the same process and then top with the 1 cup of soy cheddar shreds. Bake for 30 minutes. Serves 8.

Baked Turkey Enchiladas

 1 tablespoon olive oil
 1 pound ground turkey breast
 1 onion, chopped
 1 (10-ounce) can diced tomatoes with green chilies
 1½ cups refried beans
 ⅓ cup salsa
 ½ cup vegan Parmesan, divided
 2 brown rice tortillas

Preheat oven to 350°. Heat olive oil in a skillet on medium heat and brown the turkey breast for about 3 minutes; add the onion, tomatoes with green chilies and the refried beans. Continue cooking for about 3 minutes longer while stirring to incorporate the ingredients. Add the salsa and 4 tablespoons of the vegan Parmesan and continue cooking until the mixture is bubbly. In a 2½-quart buttered baking dish, place the tortillas and then cover with the entire turkey mixture. Sprinkle the remaining vegan Parmesan evenly over the top of casserole and bake for 30-35 minutes or until bubbly. Serves 6.

Zippy Chicken Tacos

1 (10-ounce) can diced tomatoes with green chilies
1 (10-ounce) can all white meat chicken, shredded
1 (2.25-ounce) can sliced black olives
½ teaspoon cumin
¼ teaspoon black pepper
1 (14.5-ounce) can refried beans

Brown rice tortillas or Sami's Millet & Flax Lavash

In a skillet over medium heat combine the tomatoes, chicken, black olives, cumin and black pepper. Cook 2-3 minutes; add refried beans and continue cooking until heated through. Place chicken mixture immediately onto lavash bread or brown rice tortillas. Serves 6.

Quinoa Chicken Casserole

2 cups cooked chicken pieces
1 green bell pepper, chopped
1 onion, chopped
1 can mushroom slices
2 cloves garlic, minced

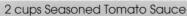
2 cups Seasoned Tomato Sauce

¾ cup cooked quinoa
1 cup vegan Parmesan

Preheat oven to 350°. In a mixing bowl combine the chicken pieces, bell pepper, onion, mushrooms and garlic. Stir to combine. Add the tomato sauce, cooked quinoa and vegan Parmesan and mix thoroughly. Pour the mixture into a buttered 2-quart baking dish and bake for 30-35 minutes or until bubbly and slightly browned. Serves 6.

Beef Stroganoff

6 tablespoons clarified butter

1 pound beef sirloin strips cut into 1-inch pieces
⅓ cup chopped sweet onion
½ pound sliced Baby Bella mushrooms
½ pound sliced button mushrooms
¼ teaspoon sea salt
⅛ teaspoon pepper
2 teaspoons wheat-free tamari
2 teaspoons chopped fresh tarragon or ½ teaspoon dried

1 cup Tofu Sour Cream
12 ounces cooked rice noodles

In a large skillet melt the clarified butter over medium heat. Stir in the beef pieces and toss to coat with the butter. Add onions and mushrooms and continue cooking until the onion is translucent and the mushrooms begin to soften. Add the sea salt, pepper and tamari and combine. Add the tarragon and remove from heat. Stir in the sour cream and serve immediately over the rice noodles. Serves 6.

Chimichanga Casserole

1 small onion, chopped

8 ounces freshly sliced mushrooms

1 tablespoon minced garlic

1¼ cups beef broth

2 tablespoons ketchup

2 tablespoons wheat-free tamari

⅛ teaspoon sea salt

 ½ cup Tofu Sour Cream

¼ teaspoon black pepper

2 brown rice tortillas

1½ pounds beef stew meat, browned

Preheat oven to 350°. In a small skillet combine the onions, mushrooms and garlic; sauté until the vegetables are softened. Set aside. In a small mixing bowl combine the beef broth, ketchup, tamari, sea salt, sour cream and pepper. Stir until the ingredients are completely mixed. In an 8-by-8-inch baking dish place a large 8-inch tortilla. Place ½ of the beef atop the tortilla, then layer ½ the vegetables and then ½ of the sour cream mixture. Repeat the process; bake for 30-35 minutes or until heated through and bubbling. Serves 6.

Pesto Pasta Skillet

 3 tablespoons basil olive oil

1 small onion, chopped

2 cloves garlic, chopped

1 pound ground turkey

2 cups chopped broccoli

1 cup chopped kale

½ teaspoon Italian seasoning

½ teaspoon sea salt

2 cups cooked brown rice pasta

1¼ cup Sun-Dried Tomato Pesto (See Sauces & Such, page 104)

In a large skillet over medium heat, place basil olive oil, onion and garlic and sauté until the onion is translucent. Add the ground turkey and continue to cook until the meat begins to brown. Add the broccoli, kale, Italian seasoning and sea salt and continue to cook until the broccoli begins to soften a bit. Gently stir in the cooked pasta and then the pesto. Continue to gently stir until all the ingredients are well combined. Cook for another 7-10 minutes or until the broccoli is tender. Serves 6.

Fresh Spinach & Sun-Dried Tomato Pesto Lasagna

3 portobello mushroom caps, chopped

5 cups loosely packed fresh spinach leaves, chopped

1 cup Sun-Dried Tomato Pesto (See Sauces & Such, page 104)

8 ounces cream cheese substitute, rice or soy at room temperature

2 tablespoons vegan Parmesan

1 large egg, slightly beaten

4 cups Seasoned Tomato Sauce

8 uncooked brown rice lasagna noodles

Preheat oven to 325°. In a mixing bowl combine the portobello mushroom caps, chopped spinach leaves and pesto. Stir together until well combined; set aside. In a small mixing bowl, combine the cream cheese, vegan Parmesan and slightly beaten egg. Stir until smooth and creamy. Pour 2 cups of the tomato sauce evenly into a buttered 9-by-13-inch baking dish. Place 4 of the uncooked lasagna noodles in a single layer on top of the sauce, top the noodles with ½ of the spinach and mushroom mixture, then place dollops of the cheese mixture atop the spinach and gently spread it evenly over the entire mixture. Place another layer of the uncooked noodles, spinach mixture and pour the remaining sauce over the top. Place the remaining cheese mixture over the sauce and gently spread it over the top evenly. Cover and bake for 1 hour or until hot and bubbly on top. Serves 8.

Carnival Squash & Sausage

2 carnival squash, peeled and cooked

1 pound country sausage, browned and drained

1 tart apple cored, peeled, sliced and cooked

1 teaspoon freshly grated nutmeg

¼ teaspoon sage

1 tablespoon olive oil

⅔ cup pure maple syrup

Salt and pepper to taste

Preheat oven to 350°. Mix together the squash, sausage and apple. Stir to combine. Stir in the nutmeg and sage and mix well. Add the olive oil and maple syrup and stir until ingredients are well combined. Add salt and pepper to taste. Bake 20 minutes or until heated through. Broil for 5-7 minutes to brown the top. Serves 4.

Salvadorian Red Beans & Ham Hocks

One year for Spanish class, my son, Wesley, completed a project on El Salvador, which had to include a recipe. He adapted this recipe, cooked it and served it to his class.

1 pound dry red beans

2 naturally smoked ham hocks

1 large sweet onion

2 teaspoons sea salt

1 teaspoon white pepper

2 teaspoons black pepper

Sami's Millet & Flax Lavash

Soy cheese shreds

Tofu Sour Cream

Rinse and soak beans overnight. In the morning, drain the beans and place in a crock pot. Add the ham hocks, onion, white and black peppers, and sea salt. Pour enough water to cover the entire mixture. Cook on low for 6 to 8 hours. Take large spoonful of ingredients and put on lavash; sprinkle soy shreds on top with a dollop of sour cream. Serves 8-10.

Veggie Lasagna

2 tablespoons garlic olive oil

5 cups coarsely shredded mixture of broccoli, cauliflower and carrots

3 cups coarsely chopped onion

10 cloves garlic, chopped

2 red bell peppers, thinly sliced

12 ounces button mushrooms, thinly sliced

8 ounces portobello mushrooms, thinly sliced

¼ teaspoon oregano

¼ teaspoon Italian seasoning

¼ teaspoon crushed rosemary

1 recipe Easy Mock Ricotta Cheese

1 lightly beaten egg

4 cups Seasoned Tomato Sauce, divided

8 uncooked brown rice lasagna noodles

Preheat oven to 350°. In a large skillet, heat garlic olive oil. Add mixture of broccoli, cauliflower and carrots. Stir and cook 3-4 minutes; add onion, chopped garlic, red bell pepper, button and portobello mushrooms. Continue cooking for an additional 5-7 minutes. Stir in the oregano, Italian seasoning and crushed rosemary. Cook another 2-3 minutes; remove from heat; set aside. In a small mixing bowl combine ricotta cheese and the lightly beaten egg and stir until blended and smooth; set aside. In a 9-by-13-inch buttered baking dish, pour 2 cups of the tomato sauce. Top the sauce with 4 of the uncooked lasagna noodles in an even layer. Top the noodles with ½ of the vegetable mixture and then the vegetables with ½ of the ricotta cheese mixture. Repeat the process. Cover and bake for 1 hour; until top is bubbly and noodles are tender when cut through. Serves 8.

Italian Buffalo Roast & Potatoes

2 (2½-pound) buffalo rump roasts

8 medium potatoes, peeled and cut into chunks

1 large sweet onion quartered

2 tablespoons chopped garlic

¾ cup diced tomatoes

½ cup water

2 cups Italian dressing of choice

Place the roast, potatoes and onion in a crock pot. Add the chopped garlic and diced tomatoes. Pour the water and the Italian dressing over over the mixture. Cook on high for 2½ hours and then turn to low and continue cooking for another 2 hours or until the roast reaches 155-160°. You may cook on low for 8 hours. Serves 8-10.

Vegetable Mai Fun

1 red bell pepper, thinly sliced

3 carrots, peeled and julienne sliced

3 celery ribs, thinly sliced

1 large onion, thinly sliced

1 tablespoon water

3 tablespoons chopped garlic

1 teaspoon freshly grated ginger

2 tablespoons olive oil

8 ounces rice stick noodles, cooked al dente

¼ cup wheat-free tamari

3 tablespoons ume plum vinegar

2 teaspoons toasted sesame oil

5 green onions, thinly sliced

In a large skillet place the red bell pepper, carrots, celery, onion and water. Cook on medium for 1-2 minutes. Add garlic and ginger; continue cooking 5-7 minutes longer until the vegetables become tender. Remove from skillet and set aside. Put olive oil in the same skillet; add cooked rice noodles. Stir 1-2 minutes to sauté lightly. Add tamari, ume plum vinegar and toasted sesame oil. Continue cooking 1-2 minutes. Pour vegetable mixture over the noodles; stir well to combine. Continue cooking 3-4 minutes until the vegetables are tender and the sauce is blended throughout the dish. Serves 6.

Sesame Orange Chicken & Broccoli

2 tablespoons blood orange olive oil

1 pound boneless, skinless chicken breast cut up

3 cups broccoli florets

4 tablespoons wheat-free tamari

1 tablespoon toasted sesame chili oil

1 small can mandarin oranges, drained with 2 tablespoons juice reserved

4 green onions, chopped

1 tablespoon toasted sesame seeds

Place the blood orange olive oil in a large skillet. Over medium heat sauté the chicken breast until it starts to whiten. Add the broccoli florets and continue cooking until the chicken loses all of its pink color. Stir in the tamari and sesame chili oil. Gently fold in the mandarin oranges and the reserved juice. Top with green onions and toasted sesame seeds. Serves 4.

Simple Beef Fajitas

1 pound lean beef steak cut into strips

1 red bell pepper, thinly sliced

2 green bell peppers, thinly sliced

2 medium onions cut into ½-inch wide chunks

2 teaspoons chopped jalapeno peppers, seeds removed

1 clove garlic, chopped

½ teaspoon cumin

¼ teaspoon sea salt

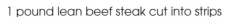
Baked Tortilla Chips

Tofu Sour Cream (optional)

Place the beef steak strips, bell peppers and onions in a large skillet over medium heat. Cook the vegetables 2-3 minutes until the onions begin to wilt. Stir in the jalapeno peppers and garlic. Continue cooking another 3-4 minutes. Add the cumin and sea salt and cook another 3-4 minutes until the vegetables are tender and the steak is tender. Serve with tortilla chips and sour cream. Serves 4.

$\mathcal{B}$aked Chicken Salad

2 cups boneless, skinless chicken breast, cooked and cubed

1 cup celery, thinly sliced

1 cup chopped water chestnuts

¾ teaspoon sea salt

¼ teaspoon pepper

2 teaspoons lemon juice

1 cups canola mayonnaise

¼ cup soy cheddar shreds

½ cup pecan pieces (optional)

½ cup Fried Onions (See Appetizers & Snacks, page 35)

Preheat oven to 350°. In mixing bowl combine the chicken breast, celery and water chestnuts. Stir in the sea salt, pepper and lemon juice. Blend well. Add the canola mayonnaise and stir the mixture to coat the chicken and vegetables. Fold in the soy cheddar shreds and pecans (if desired); top with fried onions. Place the mixture in a 9-by-9-inch buttered baking dish. Bake for 30 minutes. Serves 4.

$\mathcal{G}$arden Veggie & Rice 'Pizza'

5 cups cooked rice

3 beaten eggs

¼ cup plus 2 tablespoons vegan Parmesan

1 teaspoon garlic powder

1 orange bell pepper, thinly sliced

1 red bell pepper, thinly sliced

¾ cup chopped sweet onion

2 large tomatoes peeled and thinly sliced

1½ teaspoons garlic pepper

1 tablespoon olive oil

Preheat oven to 350°. In a large mixing bowl combine the rice, beaten eggs and ¼ cup of the vegan Parmesan and garlic powder. Blend well. Pour rice mixture onto a pizza pan and flatten it out evenly to form a crust. Top with bell peppers, onion and tomato slices. Sprinkle the top evenly with the garlic pepper and remaining vegan Parmesan. Bake for 20-25 minutes until vegetables are tender. Serves 6.

$\mathcal{M}$eaty Spinach Lasagna

1 pound ground chuck

1¼ cups chopped onion

2 tablespoons minced garlic

1 teaspoon Italian seasoning

¼ teaspoon sea salt

16 ounces frozen spinach, thawed and squeezed dry

½ cup sliced ripe olives

8 ounces cream cheese substitute, rice or soy

½ cup plus 1 tablespoon vegan Parmesan

1 egg, slightly beaten

 4½ cups Seasoned Tomato Sauce

9-10 dry rice lasagna noodles

Preheat oven to 350°. Place the ground chuck, onion, garlic, Italian seasoning and sea salt in a large skillet over medium heat. Cook until the meat is no longer pink. Drain if necessary, then stir in the spinach and olives; set aside. In a small mixing bowl combine the cream cheese substitute, vegan Parmesan and the egg. Stir until the mixture is smooth and creamy. Pour 2 cups of the tomato sauce into a 9-by-13-inch baking dish and top with 4 to 4½ lasagna noodles. Place ½ of the meat mixture atop the noodles and then top the meat with ½ the cream cheese mixture. Repeat the process; pour remaining ½ cup tomato sauce evenly over the whole dish. Sprinkle with remaining vegan Parmesan. Cover and bake for 1 hour until the noodles are tender. Serves 8.

*I*talian Pork & Potato 'Lasagna'

8 ounces fresh mushrooms, thinly sliced

1 green pepper, seeded and chopped

½ cup chopped roasted red pepper

2 tablespoons minced garlic

2 tablespoons water

¼ teaspoon sea salt

1½ cups fully cooked pork, cubed

2½ cups red potatoes, cooked and quartered

 2 cups Seasoned Tomato Sauce

2 tablespoons vegan Parmesan

1 cup soy mozzarella shreds

Preheat oven to 350°. Combine the mushrooms, green pepper, roasted red pepper and minced garlic in a large skillet over medium heat. Cook until the vegetables begin to soften. Stir in the water, sea salt and cubed pork; set aside. In a buttered 9-by-13-inch baking dish, place ½ the red potatoes then top with ½ pork mixture and 1 cup tomato sauce. Sprinkle 1 tablespoon of the vegan Parmesan and ½ cup of the soy shreds over the top of the dish. Repeat the process then bake for 35-40 minutes. Serves 8.

*B*aked Chicken & Rice with Vegetables

8 boneless chicken breast halves

1 cup bottled Italian salad dressing

1⅓ cup uncooked white rice

16 ounce mixture broccoli, carrots and water chestnuts

½ teaspoon Italian seasoning

3½ cups chicken broth

1½ cups Fried Onions (See Appetizers & Snacks, page 35)

Preheat oven to 400°. Place chicken breast halves in a 9-by-13-inch baking dish. Pour salad dressing over chicken. Bake chicken uncovered for 20 minutes. Remove from oven, place rice and vegetables around and under the chicken pieces. Sprinkle the top with Italian seasoning. Pour broth over chicken and vegetables then cook 25 minutes longer. Place fried onions on top of chicken and vegetables; bake an additional 2 minutes. Let stand 5 minutes before serving. Serves 8.

Quick Chow Mein

- 1 tablespoon olive oil
- 1 pound very lean ground beef
- ¼ teaspoon sea salt
- 1 teaspoon minced garlic
- ¼ teaspoon freshly grated ginger
- 1 cup celery, thinly sliced
- ½ cup onion, thinly sliced
- 1 cup beef broth
- 1 (7-ounce) can sliced mushrooms, drained
- 1 (8-ounce) can bamboo shoots, drained
- 1 (8-ounce) can water chestnuts, drained
- 3 tablespoons wheat-free tamari
- ¼ teaspoon xanthan gum

Heat olive oil over medium heat in a large skillet. Add ground beef, sea salt, garlic and ginger and cook until the beef is no longer pink. Add celery and onion and cook until vegetables begin to soften. Stir in the beef broth, mushrooms, bamboo shoots and water chestnuts; cover. Cook another 5 minutes or until vegetables become more tender. Stir in the tamari and xanthan gum. Continue until mixture begins to bubble and thicken. Serve with rice noodles or over brown rice. Serves 6.

Vegetable Beef Pie with Brown Rice Crust

- 2 cups cooked brown rice
- 2 eggs, beaten
- 2 tablespoons vegan Parmesan
-  ¼ cup Tofu Sour Cream
- ¼ cup cream cheese substitute, rice or soy
- ¼ pound ground beef
- 1 teaspoon minced garlic
- ¼ teaspoon black pepper
- ½ cup chopped broccoli
- ½ cup chopped carrots
- 8 ounces fresh mushrooms, sliced

Preheat oven to 350°. In a mixing bowl combine the brown rice, eggs and vegan Parmesan. Blend well; press mixture into an 8-by-8-inch baking dish to form a crust. Bake for 7-10 minutes. While crust is baking, in a mixing bowl stir together the sour cream and cream cheese; set aside. Place the ground beef and garlic in a skillet over medium heat. Cook for 2-3 minutes; add garlic, pepper, broccoli, carrots and mushrooms; continue cooking until vegetables are tender. Remove from heat; stir sour cream mixture into beef- vegetable mixture and spread out evenly. Bake for an additional 3-5 minutes to heat thoroughly; serve. Serves 4.

Flavor Tip! Use broth instead of water when cooking vegetables for extra flavor and nutrition.

One-Pot Cabbage Meal

    1 small head green cabbage, coarsely chopped
    1 pound ground turkey, browned; drained
    1 cup hot water
    ½ cup uncooked white rice
    1 cup chopped onion
    1 teaspoon sea salt
    ½ teaspoon oregano
    2 cups diced tomatoes

Preheat oven to 350°. Place cabbage in a 4-quart buttered baking dish; set aside. In a mixing bowl combine ground turkey, water, rice, onion, sea salt, oregano and tomatoes. Stir well. Pour mixture over cabbage evenly. Cover and bake 90 minutes or until rice is tender. Serves 4.

Spanish Rice

    ¼ cup canola oil
    1 medium onion, chopped
    ½ medium green pepper, chopped
    ½ pound ground beef
    1 cup uncooked white rice
    2 cups tomato sauce
    1¾ cups hot water
    1 teaspoon mustard
    1 teaspoon sea salt
    ⅛ teaspoon pepper

In a deep skillet over high heat stir together oil, onion, green pepper, ground beef and rice; cook until lightly browned. Add tomato sauce, hot water, mustard, sea salt and pepper. Bring entire mixture to a boil, stirring constantly. Cover tightly; simmer 25 minutes. Serves 4.

Pizza Stephana

    2 (12-inch) prebaked Rice Pizza Crusts (See Breads, Muffins & Crackers, page 42)
    2 tablespoons olive oil
    1 cup Greek Olive Spread (See Appetizers & Snacks, page 30)
    3 Roma tomatoes, thinly sliced
    1 bunch fresh basil, stems removed
    ½ cup vegan Parmesan

Preheat oven to 400°. Place 1 pizza crust on a pizza pan. Drizzle 1 tablespoon of olive oil over a single crust, spread ½ cup olive spread evenly on crust. Arrange ½ of the tomato slices and ½ the basil leaves appealingly on the entire pizza. Sprinkle with ¼ cup of the Parmesan. Repeat entire process for second pizza; bake for 20-22 minutes. Serves 8.

Meats

Sweet & Spicy Asian BBQ Ribs, **page 65**

Basic Meatballs

3 cups rice or sorghum cereal crumbs

2 teaspoons sea salt

2 tablespoons dried parsley

2 pounds lean ground beef

½ cup diced onion

2 tablespoons ketchup

2 tablespoons crushed garlic

3 eggs, lightly beaten

Olive oil

In a small bowl combine cereal crumbs with sea salt and parsley. In a large bowl combine beef, onions, ketchup and garlic. Add eggs, herbs and cereal crumbs to beef mixture and combine with both hands to mix well. When mixture is well combined take a small amount in hand and roll to make a 1-inch meatball. After meatballs are rolled, heat olive oil in a large frying pan and cook until all sides are nicely browned. Makes 42 meatballs.

Old Fashioned Hamburger Gravy

1 pound very lean ground beef or buffalo
8 tablespoons clarified butter
8 tablespoons brown rice flour
1½ teaspoons minced garlic
1 teaspoon garlic powder
1 teaspoon favorite salt-free blend
½ teaspoon black pepper
4 cups soy milk
Salt and pepper to taste

In a large skillet, brown ground beef or buffalo. Stir in clarified butter, brown rice flour, garlic and spices; mix well. Cook over medium heat to toast spice ingredients and blend flavors, approximately 6 minutes. Gradually stir in soy milk; continue stirring. Bring to a boil for 3-4 minutes. Reduce heat and simmer for 10-12 minutes longer. Add salt and pepper as desired. Makes approximately 6 cups.

Variation: For sausage gravy use pork sausage in place of the ground beef or buffalo and add 1 teaspoon sage to the spice ingredients.

Baked Pizza Chicken

½ cup brown rice flour
1 tablespoon garlic powder
2 tablespoons pizza seasoning
2 teaspoons sweet basil
1 cup crispy rice cereal, partially crushed
6 boneless, skinless chicken breast portions
½ cup canola oil, divided
1 (15-ounce) can fire-roasted, diced tomatoes, liquid reserved
¼ teaspoon sea salt

Preheat oven to 450°. In a medium bowl, combine brown rice flour and seasonings. Put cereal in another bowl and set aside. Trim chicken portions. In a large skillet, over medium heat, warm ¼ cup of canola oil. When oil is heated dip each chicken portion in cereal and then in flour mixture. Brown chicken portions in a skillet until both sides are crispy. In a 9-by-13-inch casserole dish, pour remaining ¼ cup canola oil to coat. Add tomatoes with liquid and sprinkle with sea salt. Place chicken portions atop tomatoes and bake for 20 minutes. Serves 6.

Meat Tip! Use tongs when turning meat on the grill. A meat fork can pierce the meat causing it to lose its natural juices.

Lemon Rosemary Chicken & Mushrooms

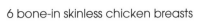

  6 bone-in skinless chicken breasts
  6 sprigs of fresh rosemary (no substitutions)
  ⅔ cup olive oil
  ⅓ cup lemon juice, freshly squeezed
  2 tablespoons garlic, crushed
  1 tablespoon fresh lemon zest
  ½ teaspoon fresh rosemary, chopped
  5 ounces shitake mushrooms, sliced

Preheat oven to 225°. On a flat surface (cutting board or marble board) place a chicken breast and one rosemary sprig. With a small sharp knife, make a small cut ¾- to 1-inch on one side of chicken portion. Feed knife through about ⅓ of chicken meat to make a slice on the other side. Remove knife and thread rosemary sprig into chicken breast through the same path made from the knife. You should be able to see both ends of the sprig. Repeat process on remaining chicken pieces. In a medium bowl, combine oil, lemon juice, garlic, lemon zest and chopped rosemary. Pour half of mixture over the chicken breasts. Cover and bake for 2 hours. Remove from oven; uncover and top with remaining juice and mushrooms. Increase oven temperature to 350°. Cover chicken and bake 30 minutes longer (removing cover halfway through) or until chicken registers 180° on meat thermometer. Serve immediately. Serves 6.

Baked Teriyaki Chicken

  4 tablespoons olive oil, divided
  6 medium chicken breasts
  1 recipe Teriyaki Sauce (See Sauces & Such, page 100)
  2 medium onions, quartered and sliced
  16 ounces fresh mushrooms, sliced

Preheat oven to 200°. Heat olive oil over medium heat in a deep skillet; brown chicken breasts. Place chicken in Teriyaki Sauce to marinate and set aside. In the same skillet heat remaining olive oil and add onions and mushrooms. Cook until vegetables are tender and set aside. Place chicken and sauce in a 9-by-13-inch pan. Cover and bake for 1 hour. Increase oven to 450°. Uncover chicken and add vegetables. Roast 15-20 minutes or until chicken registers 180° on a meat thermometer. Serve with rice or Creamy Mashed Potatoes. Serves 6.

Stuffed Beef Patties with Artichokes

  1 pound ground beef (very lean)
  1 cup natural turkey bacon, chopped and cooked
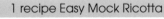 1 recipe Easy Mock Ricotta
  1 tablespoon olive oil
  1 onion, thinly sliced
  5 ounces mushrooms, quartered
  1 (11½-ounce) jar marinated artichoke hearts with liquid
  ¼ cup balsamic vinegar

Preheat oven to 350°. Divide ground beef into 8 equal portions and roll into balls. Flatten meatballs into 8 even-sized patties. On each patty, place ¼ cup natural turkey bacon pieces and 1 tablespoon ricotta. Place a second patty on top of first. Flatten the top patty over the bottom one and pinch edges together so they won't separate. Place patties in a 9-by-9-inch baking dish and bake for 15 minutes. While patties are baking, heat olive oil in a 10-inch skillet over medium heat. Add onion slices and mushrooms; cook 2-3 minutes or until onion is translucent. Add artichoke hearts and balsamic vinegar. Continue to cook for 4-5 minutes longer. Set aside. Remove beef patties and cover with vegetables. Cover dish and bake for 30 minutes longer. Serves 4.

Curry & Dill Chicken Breasts

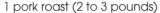

2 tablespoons clarified butter
2 tablespoons Basic Baking Mix
⅛ teaspoon sea salt
Black pepper to taste
1 cup soy milk
¼ cup canola mayonnaise
½ teaspoon dill weed
¼ teaspoon curry powder
6 bone-in chicken breast halves
1 tablespoon canola oil

Preheat oven to 350°. In a saucepan over medium heat, melt clarified butter and slowly add baking mix, sea salt and pepper. Stir gently. Gradually add soy milk stirring constantly. Bring to a boil and continue to stir for 2 more minutes. Remove from heat, add mayonnaise, dill and curry; stir until sauce is smooth. Set aside. In a large skillet, brown chicken portions in canola oil. Place chicken in a 3-quart baking dish. Pour sauce over chicken and bake uncovered for 50-60 minutes or until the chicken juices run clear. Serves 6.

Pork Roast Dinner

1 pork roast (2 to 3 pounds)
6-7 medium red potatoes
1½ pounds baby carrots
3 onions, cut into fourths
3 celery ribs, cut into halves
1 tablespoon garlic powder
1 tablespoon basil
½ tablespoon salt-free blend
½ tablespoon rosemary, crushed
½ tablespoon sea salt
2 cups water

Preheat oven to 350°. In a large roasting pan, brown the pork roast on all sides over medium heat. Add the potatoes, carrots, onions and celery to the pan. Sprinkle the garlic powder, basil, salt-free blend, rosemary and sea salt over the roast and vegetables evenly. Pour the 2 cups of water over the meat and vegetables. Bake for 1 hour or until vegetables are fork tender and a meat thermometer registers 165°. Allow meat to rest 20-30 minutes before carving. Serves 10.

Skillet Chicken with Honey Mustard Glaze

½ teaspoon olive oil
4 boneless, skinless chicken breasts, butterflied
2 small sweet onions, thinly sliced
¼ teaspoon sea salt
⅛ teaspoon pepper
1 recipe Honey Mustard Glaze (See Sauces & Such, page 102)

Heat olive oil over medium heat in a large skillet. Add chicken breasts and cook until the sides are slightly browned. Reduce the heat to low and add the onions. Sprinkle the mixture with the sea salt and pepper and cover. Continue cooking the mixture until the onions begin to soften, 5-6 minutes. Pour the Honey Mustard Glaze over the chicken and onions. Increase the cooking temperature to medium, and bring the mixture to a soft boil. Reduce the heat and simmer, uncovered for 18-20 minutes or until the chicken and onions are very tender. Serves 4.

Italian Sirloin Tip Roast

1 (2½-pound) sirloin tip roast
1 (14.5-ounce) can diced tomatoes
1 (28-ounce) can crushed tomatoes
1 tablespoon Italian seasoning
2 teaspoons favorite salt-free blend
1 head garlic, cloves peeled and broken
⅓ cup water
½ teaspoon sea salt

Place all ingredients in a crock pot and stir lightly to blend tomatoes and herbs. Cook on low for 4-4½ hours. Serves 8.

Cider Grilled Chicken

3 pounds boneless, skinless, chicken breasts
4 cups apple cider
2 cloves garlic, chopped
1 teaspoon thyme
1 onion, thinly sliced

Slice each chicken breast in half. Place each portion in a deep 9-by-13-inch glass baking dish and set aside. In a mixing bowl stir together the apple cider, chopped garlic and thyme. Pour mixture over the chicken portions and top with the sliced onion. Cover and place in the refrigerator for at least 2 hours. Remove chicken portions from the dish and grill on medium for 10 minutes, turn and continue grilling until pieces have an internal temperature of 180°. While the chicken is grilling, pour the marinade into a large saucepan and bring to a boil. Reduce heat and simmer uncovered for 15 minutes. Remove onion pieces and set aside, then strain liquid mixture and reserve mixture in a 4-cup liquid measure. Place grilled chicken pieces in a deep serving dish, top with cooked onion pieces and liquid mixture and serve. Serves 12.

Flavor Tip! When cooking rice, use broth instead of water to boost the flavor.

Coating for Oven-Fried Pork, Chicken or Fish

¾ cup rice bread crumbs

2 teaspoons garlic powder

1 teaspoon sea salt

1½ teaspoons paprika

1 teaspoon Italian seasoning

Place all ingredients in a gallon-size resealable bag and shake the bag to mix ingredients. Place meat portions in the bag, one piece at a time, closing the bag tightly and shaking the meat portion in the mixture until completely coated. Coating will adequately cover approximately 2 pounds of meat.

Fiesta Chicken Loaf

2 pounds ground chicken

1 (4.25-ounce) can chopped black olives

3 tablespoons minced garlic

1 cup chopped onion

2 cups rice bread crumbs

1 cup salsa

3 eggs, slightly beaten

¾ teaspoon cumin

Preheat oven to 350°. In a large mixing bowl place the ground chicken, chopped black olives and minced garlic. Mix ingredients with a large spoon or hands until they are well combined. Add the onion and rice bread crumbs and mix again until incorporated. Add the salsa, eggs and cumin and mix thoroughly. Divide the chicken mixture into two equal portions and shape them into loaf forms. Place portions in 2 loaf pans and bake for 35-40 minutes or cover and freeze one for use at a later time. Each loaf serves 4.

Sweet & Spicy Asian BBQ Ribs

2 full racks of baby back ribs, trimmed

2 (8.5-ounce) bottles wheat-free hoisin sauce

8 tablespoons water

½ cup honey

2 tablespoons chopped garlic

1 teaspoon chili-garlic sauce

Preheat oven to 300°. In a roasting pan, place ribs and cover lightly. Bake for 2 hours. While the ribs are baking, combine the hoisin sauce, water, honey, chopped garlic and chili-garlic sauce in a small mixing bowl and blend well. Remove the ribs from the oven and pour ½ the sauce mixture over them. Continue to bake for 30 minutes, basting with the sauce every 10 minutes and covering with the remaining sauce before the last 10 minutes of cooking. Serves 6.

Herb Roasted Chicken & Potatoes

1 roasting chicken (3½ to 5 pounds)
1 tablespoon freshly chopped oregano
2 teaspoons freshly chopped thyme
1 tablespoon freshly chopped rosemary
5 garlic cloves, finely chopped
8 fresh basil leaves, divided
1 onion, peeled and quartered
2 tablespoons olive oil
1 teaspoon sea salt
½ teaspoon freshly ground pepper
6 baking potatoes quartered lengthwise

Preheat oven to 450°. Remove and discard giblets from chicken. Rinse the chicken thoroughly with cold water and pat dry. Trim off excess fat. Beginning at the neck cavity, loosen skin from breast and drumsticks by carefully inserting fingertips. Combine the oregano, thyme, rosemary and garlic. Rub the herb and garlic blend underneath the loosened skin. Carefully place 5 of the basil leaves underneath the loosened skin. Tie the ends of legs with cord lifting wing tips up and over to tuck under chicken. Place chicken, breast side up on a buttered broiler pan. Place the quartered onion in the breast cavity with the remaining 3 basil leaves. Rub the olive oil over the chicken skin and sprinkle with sea salt and pepper. Insert a meat thermometer into the meaty part of thigh making sure not to touch the bone. Bake for 30 minutes. Reduce temperature to 350°, remove chicken and arrange potatoes around it on pan. Place back in oven and cook another 45 minutes or until the chicken temperature on the meat thermometer reads 180°. Allow meat to rest 5 minutes before serving. Serves 6 – 10.

Herb Marinated Lamb Chops

4 lamb chops approximately ½ inch thick
½ cup canola oil
¼ cup chopped onion
 ¼ cup red wine vinegar
½ cup dry red wine
1 clove garlic, minced
1 teaspoon sea salt
½ teaspoon rosemary, crushed
½ teaspoon thyme
¼ teaspoon pepper

Trim the lamb chops and place one or two small slits on the underside to keep from curling during broiling time; set aside. In a large glass mixing bowl combine the canola oil, onion, vinegar, red wine, garlic, sea salt, rosemary, thyme and pepper. Stir to combine. Place the lamb chops in a large resealable bag. Pour the oil and vinegar mixture into the bag. Place the bag in the refrigerator and marinate for at least 6 hours, turning periodically to ensure flavor throughout. After the chops are marinated, place them on a broiler pan, reserving ¼ cup of marinade. Broil 3 inches from the heat for 5-6 minutes. Turn; brush with remaining marinade and continue broiling for an additional 5-6 minutes or to desired temperature. Serves 4.

New York Roast

I reserve this roast for holidays, special occasions or family gatherings.

 1 (5-pound) New York strip loin roast
 4 cloves garlic
 4 tablespoon olive oil
 1 tablespoon plus 2 teaspoons sea salt
 2 tablespoons freshly ground pepper

Preheat oven to 450°. Cut 4 small, deep slits in the loin roast and insert one garlic clove into each slit. Rub the entire roast with the olive oil, then cover it with the salt and freshly ground pepper, patting it onto the meat so that it adheres to the outside. Let the roast stand at room temperature for 30 minutes. Place in a roasting pan with fat side up and cook for 20 minutes. Decrease oven temperature to 350° and continue roasting to desired temperature. The ideal temperature for this roast is 130°. Allow meat to rest for 15 minutes before slicing to serve. It takes approximately 1 hour and 45 minutes to cook the roast to a doneness of medium. Serves 18.

Horseradish Buffalo Roast

 1 large cooking bag
 1 tablespoon sorghum flour
 1 (2- to 2½-pound) buffalo roast
 1 (5-ounce) jar horseradish (not sauce)
 Sea salt and pepper to taste
 3 cloves garlic, halved
  3 tablespoons garlic olive oil
 8 carrots, sliced (peel if desired)
 6 medium potatoes, quartered
 1 cup water
 3 onions, cut into halves
 1 (14.5-ounce) can diced tomatoes

Preheat oven to 325°. Shake flour in cooking bag and place bag in roasting pan. Spread horseradish on both sides of roast. YES, the entire jar! Place roast in bag, add salt and pepper to taste, garlic, olive oil, vegetables, tomatoes and water. Close bag and poke a few holes in the top. Bake for 2 hours or until meat falls from the bone and is fork tender. Serve on a platter with the broth from pan. Serves 8.

Flat Iron Steak

A flat iron steak is a cut that does best if it's not cooked to a temperature higher than 160°, which is medium doneness. I like it best when cooked between 150-155°.

1 pound flat iron steak
2 tablespoons basil olive oil
4 cloves garlic, crushed
2 teaspoon parsley
1 teaspoon rosemary, crushed
½ teaspoon dry mustard
¼ cup dry red wine
2 large yellow onions, thinly sliced
12 ounces fresh mushrooms, thinly sliced

In a resealable gallon bag place the steak, basil olive oil and crushed garlic. Crush bag to combine ingredients. Add the parsley, rosemary and dry mustard and crush bag again to combine. Pour red wine over the mixture, seal the bag and refrigerate for at least 2 hours. After the meat has marinated, place steak in a large skillet preheated on medium heat, reserving liquid. Place onion and mushroom slices around the steak; cover and cook for 5-7 minutes. Turn steak and continue to cook, adding reserved liquid in tablespoon portions as needed to keep meat from becoming too brown. Continue cooking until a meat thermometer reads medium rare. Slice steak in diagonal strips and serve with onions and mushrooms on the side. Serves 4.

Gourmet Buffalo Burgers

1½ pounds ground buffalo
½ pound ground chuck (beef)
½ cup chopped onion
½ teaspoon basil
½ teaspoon sea salt
1 tablespoon chopped garlic
⅓ cup cream cheese substitute, rice or soy

In a bowl, combine the buffalo and beef. Add the onion, basil, sea salt and garlic. Mix thoroughly by hand until completely combined. Stir in the cream cheese substitute and mix again until completely combined. Divide the meat mixture into 8 equal portions. Roll each portion into a ball and then flatten out by hand forming a burger. Grill, fry or broil burgers to desired doneness. Serves 8.

Pork Cutlets with Mushroom Gravy

1 pound pork cutlets
⅓ cup plus 2 tablespoons sorghum flour, divided
½ teaspoon favorite salt-free blend
½ teaspoon garlic salt
3 tablespoons canola margarine, divided
8 ounces fresh mushrooms, sliced
2 tablespoons water
1 cup soy milk

Season to taste. after mixture

Lay the pork cutlets on a plate; set aside. In a small bowl combine ⅓ cup of the sorghum flour, salt-free blend and garlic salt. Sprinkle each cutlet with enough of the flour mixture to coat completely, turn each cutlet and repeat. In a preheated skillet, place 1 tablespoon of the canola margarine. Stir in the mushrooms and cook for about 1 minute. Push the mushrooms to the sides of the pan with a spatula and place the pork cutlets in the skillet. Cook on medium high heat until the cutlets are nicely browned on one side. Turn over the cutlets and repeat browning. Reduce heat to medium and allow to cook for about 5-8 minutes or until the cutlets are cooked entirely. Remove the cutlets from the pan and set aside. Place the water in the skillet and stir it well to deglaze the pan. Add the remaining canola margarine and sorghum flour and stir to coat the mushrooms. Gently stir in the soy milk and continue to cook until bubbly and it begins to thicken. Place the cutlets back in the pan and stir to coat the cutlets with the gravy mixture. Heat through and serve. Serves 4.

Country-Style Oven-Fried Chicken Strips

2 pounds boneless, skinless, chicken breast cut into even strips

2 tablespoons canola mayonnaise

¾ cup soy milk

1 cup rice bread crumbs

3 tablespoons vegan Parmesan

1 teaspoon garlic powder

¼ teaspoon sea salt

⅛ teaspoon pepper

Place chicken strips in a glass bowl; set aside. In a small bowl combine the canola mayonnaise and the soy milk. Stir until smooth. Pour the mixture over the chicken strips; cover and refrigerate for at least 1 hour. In another small bowl combine the rice bread crumbs, vegan Parmesan, garlic powder, sea salt and pepper. Stir to combine ingredients. After the chicken has marinated for the appropriate time preheat oven to 400° and remove chicken from refrigerator. Carefully dip each chicken piece into the crumb mixture to coat completely. Place the coated strips on a shallow baking sheet with none overlapping. Bake for 12-15 minutes or until the juices run clear and meat is tender. Serves 8.

Crispy Roast Duck

1 duck (5 to 6 pounds)

2 cups boiling water

1 tablespoon sea salt

1 teaspoon freshly ground pepper

2 teaspoons minced garlic

Preheat oven to 425°. Cut off wing tips of duck with a sharp knife and discard. Remove and discard excess fat from duck's neck and body cavity, then rinse the duck thoroughly inside and out. Prick the skin of the duck all over with a fork then fold the skin of the neck under the body. Place duck, breast side up, on a roasting rack in a 9-by-13-inch baking pan. Pour boiling water over the duck to tighten the skin. Cool; pour out excess water from duck cavity into pan. Pat duck dry inside and out reserving liquid in pan. Rub the duck with the sea salt, ground pepper and garlic. Roast breast side up for 45 minutes; remove, turn duck and roast 45 minutes longer. Remove and turn duck again; roast an additional 45 minutes until the skin of the duck is brown and crisp. Remove from oven, drain any excess liquid from cavity and allow to rest 15 minutes before carving. Serves 4.

Salsa Chicken

6 boneless, skinless chicken breasts cut into even portions

2 cups Confetti Salsa (See Sauces & Such, page103)

1 (4-ounce) can chopped green chilies

½ teaspoon garlic salt

1 can sliced black olives

1 cup soy cheddar shreds

½ cup Tofu Sour Cream

Baked Tortilla Chips

In a preheated skillet, place chicken portions. Cook over medium heat for 3-4 minutes, turn chicken and continue cooking until the second side begins to brown. Stir in salsa, green chilies, garlic salt and black olives. Continue cooking until chicken is cooked through and tender. Top with soy cheddar shreds and sour cream. Serve with additional salsa and tortilla chips. Serves 6.

Sweet Italian Sausage & Sauerkraut

6 turkey Italian sausages, cut in half

2 small apples, peeled and chopped

4 tablespoons sucanat

3 tablespoons apple cider vinegar

2 tablespoons water

16 ounces sauerkraut rinsed and drained 3-4 times

1 tablespoon spicy brown mustard

In a deep skillet over medium heat, brown the Italian sausage halves and continue to cook until they are no longer pink and cooked through. Remove from skillet; set aside. In the same skillet, place the chopped apples, sucanat, vinegar and water. Heat until bubbly, then reduce heat to low and cover. Cook 2-3 minutes longer. Add sauerkraut and brown mustard. Stir well to combine. Cover skillet and cook for another 15-20 minutes on low heat. Add sausage halves, increase heat to medium and cook an additional 5-7 minutes or until heated thoroughly. Serves 6.

Zesty Potato Meatloaf

2 cups Creamy Mashed Potatoes

2 pounds lean ground beef

¾ cup soy milk

1 large onion, chopped

2 cloves garlic, minced

¾ cup salsa, divided

⅛ teaspoon sea salt

⅛ teaspoon pepper

Preheat oven to 350°. In a mixing bowl combine the mashed potatoes, ground beef and soy milk. Mix well; add onion, garlic, ½ cup of the salsa, sea salt and pepper. Stir or mix with hands to incorporate ingredients. Form meat mixture into a loaf and place in loaf pan; top with remaining ¼ cup salsa. Bake for 45-60 minutes. Serves 8.

Quick & Easy Skillet Steak

1 pound thinly sliced skillet steak
8 ounces fresh mushrooms, sliced
2 tablespoons wheat-free tamari, divided
1 teaspoon favorite salt-free blend
1 teaspoon canola oil
1 tablespoon soy flour
⅔ cup soymilk

In a skillet over medium heat, place the sliced steak pieces and mushrooms. Cook for 2-3 minutes; add 1 tablespoon of the wheat-free tamari and salt-free blend. Continue cooking another 1-2 minutes or until the steak strips are browned completely. Remove steak and mushrooms from skillet; set aside. Stir in the canola oil; add soy flour and stir to brown slightly. Add remaining tamari and gently stir in soy milk. Bring to a boil, stirring constantly. Return steak and mushrooms to skillet and cook until heated thoroughly. Serves 4.

Bacon Tip! Heat oven to 375° and cook bacon on a broiler pan for 12-17 minutes or until desired crispness. This method turns out perfect bacon and creates less mess.

Fish & Seafood

Lemon Dill Tilapia, **page 77**

Tuna Zucchini Frittata

- 1 tablespoon olive oil
- 1 onion, chopped
- 1 small zucchini, thinly sliced
- 1 red bell pepper, seeded and sliced
- 2 tablespoons soy milk
- 4 eggs
- 2 tablespoons soy milk
- 1 (7-ounce) can all white tuna in water, drained
- 2 teaspoons herbs de Provence (a purchased blend of French herbs)
- Sea salt
- Black pepper
- ½ cup soy cheddar shreds

Preheat broiler to 500°. Heat olive oil in a large oven-safe skillet over medium heat. Add onions, zucchini and red bell pepper and cook for 5 minutes. In another bowl, beat eggs with soy milk. Add tuna, herbs, sea salt and pepper to taste. Mix well and then pour egg mixture over vegetables. Cook over medium heat until eggs begin to set. Pull the sides of eggs to the middle to allow uncooked egg to run onto the pan. Continue cooking until the frittata is golden brown underneath. When finished, top it with the cheese and place it under the broiler for 2-3 minutes or until golden brown. Serve immediately. Serves 4-6.

Asian Noodles & Shrimp

    10-12 ounces frozen cooked shrimp
    2 tablespoons canola oil
    3 carrots, sliced in diagonal coins
    3 celery ribs, cut up
    3 leeks, thinly sliced
    3 tablespoons chopped garlic
    1½ teaspoons fresh ginger root, chopped
    ⅛ teaspoon white pepper
    1 tablespoon potato starch flour
    10-12 ounces thin rice noodles, cooked
    5 tablespoons wheat-free tamari
    3-4 scallions, chopped

In a colander, thaw shrimp, remove tails, rinse and drain. Set aside. In a large sauté pan heat canola oil and add carrots; sauté 2-3 minutes then add celery and leeks. Cook until wilted. Add garlic and ginger root and sauté another 2-3 minutes. Add white pepper and stir in potato starch flour, stirring until browned, 1-2 minutes. Add rice noodles and toss. Then pour in tamari and stir. Cook 1-2 minutes longer; top with scallions and serve. Serves 4.

Herb & Citrus Whitefish

    1 lime, juiced
    ½ lemon, juiced
    3 tablespoons chopped garlic
    2 tablespoons honey
    1½ tablespoons tarragon
    ⅛ teaspoon marjoram
    ½ teaspoon white pepper
    6 medium whitefish fillets, washed and patted dry
    4 scallions, chopped

Preheat oven to 400°. Place lime and lemon juices in a small bowl; add garlic and honey. Add herbs; mix well. In a 9-by-9-inch buttered baking dish, lay out the fillets. Place a spoonful of citrus mixture over each fillet. Bake for 20-25 minutes. Remove from oven when fish is flakey and opaque. Top with scallions before serving. Serves 6.

Whitefish with Mustard Sauce

    4 whitefish fillets, washed and patted dry, 3-4 ounces each (hake, cod etc.)
    ¼ cup olive oil
    1 tablespoon minced garlic
    1 tablespoon stone ground mustard

Preheat oven to 400°. Lay fillets in an 8-by-8-inch baking pan. In a liquid measure, combine olive oil, garlic and mustard. Whisk to blend. Spread sauce evenly over each fillet. Bake 10-15 minutes or until fish is flakey and opaque. Serves 4.

Salmon Patties

12 ounces boneless pink salmon

¼ cup finely chopped onion

2 tablespoons brown rice flour

2 eggs

½ cup potato chip crumbs

1 teaspoon mustard

2 tablespoons wheat-free tamari

1 teaspoon thyme

Drain salmon and place in a bowl. Add all other ingredients to the salmon. Mix well with a wooden spoon or your hands. Form into 6 equal size patties. Fry, over medium heat, in a 12-inch nonstick skillet until golden brown on both sides. Makes 6 patties.

Honey Pecan Salmon

½ cup honey

2 tablespoons canola oil

½ cup toasted pecans, coarsely chopped

4 equally sized salmon fillets, washed and patted dry (about 1½ pounds total)

½ teaspoons sea salt

Preheat oven to 425°. In a saucepan combine honey, canola oil and toasted pecans. Cook over medium-high heat until the pecans are completely coated. Remove sauce; cover and keep warm. Place salmon fillets in a 9-by-9-inch baking dish; sprinkle with sea salt. Pour sauce over fillets. Cover dish loosely with foil. Bake 7-10 minutes or until fish is flakey and opaque. Serves 4.

Breaded Catfish Nuggets

1 cup pecan meal

1 cup amaranth flour

1 tablespoon garlic powder

¼ teaspoon black pepper

1 teaspoon sea salt

1 pound fresh catfish nuggets, washed and patted dry

Canola oil

Combine pecan meal, amaranth flour and spices in a bowl. Dip each fish portion into mix and generously cover. Fry in canola oil until fish nuggets flake easily. Serves 4.

Shrimp & Vegetables

1 (12-ounce) package of frozen cooked shrimp, thawed and tails removed

2 tablespoon clarified butter

1 medium onion, cut into medium sized pieces.

2 tablespoons chopped garlic

1 (14½-ounce) can diced tomatoes

1 (6-ounce) jar of marinated artichokes, chopped with liquid

1 (8-ounce) can water chestnuts, chopped

1 (14.4-ounce) can bean sprouts (or ½ cup fresh)

2 tablespoons wheat-free tamari

In a colander, rinse shrimp thoroughly and set aside. In a large skillet, over medium heat, melt clarified butter and add onion and garlic. Cook until the onion is translucent. Add diced tomatoes, artichokes, water chestnuts, bean sprouts and tamari. Stir and cook for 1-2 minutes. Add shrimp and toss together until heated through. Serve over rice. Serves 4.

 alsa Baked Cod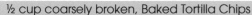

1½ pounds cod, washed and patted dry

1 cup salsa

1 cup soy cheddar shreds

 ½ cup coarsely broken, Baked Tortilla Chips

1 recipe Guacamole (See Appetizers & Snacks, page 30)

Preheat oven to 400°. Rinse cod fillets and pat dry. Lay fillets in a buttered 9-by-13-inch casserole dish. Pour salsa over fillets so that they are covered evenly. Bake for 15 minutes, then remove dish from oven and sprinkle fillets with the soy cheddar shreds evenly. Place back in the oven for 5-7 minutes or until fillets become opaque and flake easily with a fork. Sprinkle tortilla chips over the top of the fillets and serve with guacamole. Serves 6

 omato & Scallop Pasta

10 ounces fettuccine-style rice noodles, cooked

4 tablespoons olive oil

1 tablespoon crushed garlic

1 cup chopped carrots

1 cup chopped onions

1 (15-ounce) can diced tomatoes

½ teaspoon sea salt

1½ pound sea scallops

In a large sauté pan heat olive oil; add garlic, then carrots and onions. Cook over medium heat until carrots begin to soften and onions are translucent. Add diced tomatoes and sea salt and continue to cook 3-5 minutes longer. Add sea scallops and continue cooking until scallops turn white and are firm throughout. Add noodles and toss to blend mixture. Drizzle with additional 2 tablespoons of olive oil, stir and serve. Serves 6.

armesan Dill Whitefish

4 whitefish fillets, rinsed and patted dry

½ lemon, juiced

¼ teaspoon sea salt

¼ cup vegan Parmesan

1 tablespoon chopped dill, stems removed

Preheat oven to 400°. Place fillets in a shallow baking pan. Pour lemon juice evenly over fillets and then sprinkle with sea salt. Evenly distribute the vegan Parmesan and chopped dill over the fillets. Bake 20-22 minutes or until fish is flakey and opaque. Serves 4.

Baked Orange Roughy with Tomatoes & Mushrooms

- 1 pound orange roughy fillets, rinsed and patted dry
- 4 sprigs fresh dill, stems removed
- 2 fresh tomatoes cut into wedges
- 4 ounces fresh mushrooms, sliced

Preheat oven to 450°. Place the fillets in a shallow baking dish and top each one with a sprig of the fresh dill. Arrange the tomato wedges and the mushrooms around the fillets to evenly cover the bottom of the pan. Bake 18-20 minutes or until the fish is flakey and opaque. Serves 4.

Salmon Kabobs

- 1 large red bell pepper
- 1 large green bell pepper
- 1 pound salmon fillets cut into 1-inch cubes
- 4 wooden skewers soaked in water for at least 10 minutes
- 1 teaspoon sea salt
- ½ teaspoon freshly ground black pepper
- 1½ tablespoons olive oil

Preheat oven to 425°. Core and seed the red and green peppers; then cut them into 1-inch squares. On each skewer thread a cube of salmon, red pepper, salmon, green pepper until the skewer is full. Repeat process on remaining skewers. Place the completed skewers on a baking sheet and sprinkle with sea salt and black pepper evenly. Drizzle olive oil evenly over each kabob. Bake for 15-17 minutes; until the salmon flakes. Serves 4.

Crispy Oven-Baked Whitefish

- ¾ cup rice cereal crumbs
- ¼ cup sorghum flour
- 2 teaspoons garlic powder
- 1 teaspoon paprika
- ½ teaspoon sea salt
- 4 whitefish fillets, washed and patted dry

Preheat oven to 400°. In a small bowl combine the cereal crumbs, sorghum flour, garlic powder, paprika and sea salt. Dip each white fish fillet into crumb mixture until completely coated. Place the coated fillets in a 9–by–13-inch baking dish and bake for 12-14 minutes or until fish flakes nicely with a fork. Serves 4.

Pecan Crusted Salmon

- 1 cup finely chopped pecans
- ⅔ cup rice bread crumbs
- ½ teaspoon sea salt
- 4 tablespoons canola mayonnaise
- 4 (6-ounce) salmon fillets, rinsed, patted dry

Preheat oven to 375°. In a small bowl combine pecans, bread crumbs and sea salt; set aside. Spread both sides of each salmon fillet with 1 tablespoon of the mayonnaise. Dip each fillet into the crumb mixture to coat nicely. Place in a shallow baking pan and bake for 12-16 minutes, depending upon the thickness of the fillets or until the fish flakes nicely with a fork. Note: Salmon should be baked approximately 10 minutes at 375° for every inch of thickness of the fillet. Serves 4.

Lemon Dill Tilapia

- 1 pound tilapia fillets rinsed, patted dry
- 2 fresh lemons
- 1 teaspoon paprika
- ¼ teaspoon freshly ground black pepper
- 4 teaspoons freshly chopped dill
- Olive oil
- Fresh dill fronds for garnish

Preheat oven to 350°. Line a 9-by-13-inch baking pan with foil. Place the tilapia fillets in the pan; set aside. Thinly slice one of the lemons; set aside. Juice the second lemon and pour juice evenly over the fish fillets. In a small bowl combine the paprika, black pepper, and freshly chopped dill and stir to combine; set aside. Drizzle the fish fillets with olive oil then sprinkle the paprika mixture evenly over each fillet. Top each fillet with 1 or 2 slices of fresh lemon and bake for 10-12 minutes; until fish flakes easily with a fork. Garnish with dill fronds; serve. Serves 4.

Shrimp & Veggie Mai Fun

- 2 tablespoons minced garlic
- ⅓ cup chopped carrot
- 1 tablespoon water
- 1 onion, thinly sliced
- 1 red bell pepper, thinly sliced
- 3 cups broccoli florets
- 1 pound raw shrimp, deveined with tails removed
- 2 tablespoons olive oil
- 2½ cups rice noodles cooked, but firm
- ½ teaspoon white pepper
- 2 teaspoons freshly grated ginger
- 2 tablespoons ume plum vinegar
- 2 teaspoons toasted sesame oil

Place garlic and carrot in a large skillet over medium heat. Cook until the sugar in the carrot begins to caramelize; stir in water. Add the onion, bell pepper and broccoli and continue cooking until the vegetables begin to soften. Stir in the shrimp and cook an additional 3-5 minutes until the shrimp has changed to a pinkish, coral color. Pour mixture from the skillet into a large mixing bowl; set aside. In the same skillet, heat the olive oil; stir in the rice noodles. Cook for 2 minutes then add the white pepper, ginger, ume plum vinegar and toasted sesame oil. Stir to combine ingredients. Stir the vegetable and shrimp mixture into the noodles to combine well. Continue cooking until heated thoroughly; serve. Serves 8.

Vegetables

Pesto Pasta Skillet, **page 52**

Baked Red Onions

        6 large red onions, all similar in size
        1 tablespoon olive oil
        ¼ cup pine nuts
        ¼ cup vegan Parmesan
        ⅓ cup toasted rice bread crumbs
        1½ teaspoons ground coriander
        ⅛ teaspoon sea salt
        Pepper to taste

Preheat oven to 350°. Peel onions and remove a thin slice from both top and bottom of onions. Place onions in a pot of boiling water and cook them until tender (13-15 minutes). Drain onions and scoop out inside part of the onion leaving 3 or so layers of the onion for a shell. Place onion shells in a buttered 4-quart glass baking dish. Chop inner part of the onion that was removed and set aside. In a 10-inch skillet, over medium heat, heat olive oil and cook chopped onions and pine nuts until they are golden brown. Place vegan Parmesan in a bowl and stir in onion mixture to blend. Add toasted bread crumbs, coriander and sea salt. Spoon Parmesan mixture evenly into onion shells and add pepper to taste. Cover dish and bake for 25 minutes; uncover and bake 10 minutes longer until golden brown. Serves 6.

Savory Potato Fries

        2 teaspoons sea salt
        1 tablespoon garlic powder
        ⅛ teaspoon black pepper
        1½ teaspoons crushed thyme
        7 baking potatoes
        ¼ cup canola oil

Preheat oven to 375°. Combine the first four ingredients in a small bowl and set aside. Wash and scrub the potatoes. Leaving skins intact, cut into halves and then halves again the long way. Then cut potatoes into stick like pieces resembling french fries. Rinse all of the potatoes and pat dry with a paper towel. Place potatoes into a large bowl and cover with canola oil; stir in the spice mixture to coat well. Put potatoes on a large cookie sheet or jelly roll pan in one layer and bake for 20 minutes. Remove pan, turn potatoes and bake for 15 minutes longer or until the potatoes are tender and golden brown. Serves 6.

Glazed Green Beans

        1 pound frozen baby green beans
        1½ tablespoons clarified butter
        ⅓ cup apricot 100% fruit spread
        ⅛ teaspoon sea salt

Steam green beans until they are tender. In a glass bowl mix fruit spread, clarified butter and sea salt. Heat uncovered in a microwave on high for 25-30 seconds. Place beans in a serving dish and stir in fruit mixture until coated. Serves 4.

Fast & Fancy Brussels Sprouts

    2 bags frozen Brussels sprouts, thawed
    ½ package natural turkey bacon, chopped
    1 medium onion, chopped
    ½ cup water
    ½ cup dried cranberries

Brown the turkey bacon and onion in a large skillet. Add the thawed Brussels sprouts and water. Cook on medium heat for 15 minutes or until the Brussels sprouts are tender. Stir in the dried cranberries and mix well. Serves 8.

Italian Stir-Fry Vegetables

    1 large sweet onion, cut into medium-sized pieces
    2 tablespoons chopped garlic
    3 potatoes, peeled and thinly sliced
    1 green bell pepper, seeded and cut into medium-sized pieces
    1 yellow bell pepper, seeded and cut into medium-sized pieces
    8 ounces fresh mushrooms, sliced
    ¼ teaspoon garlic pepper
    ¾ teaspoon Italian seasoning
    2 tomatoes, peeled and chopped
    1 (15.5-ounce) can cannellini beans

In a large skillet cook onion and garlic on medium heat until onion begins to soften. Add potato slices and continue cooking for 5-6 minutes. Add the green and yellow bell pepper and cook for another 3 minutes. Stir in the mushroom slices, garlic pepper and Italian seasoning. Continue cooking for 2-3 minutes longer or until vegetables are tender. Stir in tomatoes and cannellini beans and continue cooking until heated through. Serves 6.

Creamy Cauliflower

    1½ quarts water
    7 cups cauliflower florets
    ⅓ cup canola mayonnaise
    ⅛ teaspoon sea salt
    ⅓ cup vegan Parmesan
    1 teaspoon parsley flakes

Cook cauliflower until tender and drain reserving 3 tablespoons of the water. Place the cooked cauliflower and the 3 tablespoons of water in a blender. Add mayonnaise and blend well. Add sea salt and pulse several times to mix. Add vegan Parmesan and blend well, until the mixture is creamy. Pour cauliflower mixture into a serving bowl, sprinkle with parsley flakes. Serves 6.

Wonderfully Wilted Greens

½ package natural turkey bacon

½ cup, plus 2 tablespoons water

2 cups red chard, cut into 1- to 2-inch pieces with stems removed

6 cups mixed baby greens

1 large sweet onion, chopped

¼ cup apple cider vinegar

2-3 tablespoons sucanat (amount depends on amount of sweetness preferred)

Chop the turkey bacon into small pieces and brown over medium heat. While the turkey bacon is browning, place red chard, greens and onion into a large bowl and set aside. Remove the turkey bacon from the pan when it is browned. Add 2 tablespoons of the water to the pan and keep cooking to deglaze the pan. Remove from heat and set aside. In a small saucepan place vinegar, sucanat and remaining water. Stir well, then bring the mixture to a rolling boil. Add turkey bacon and water. Pour hot dressing mixture over the greens and onions to wilt. Stir gently and serve. Serves 4.

Roasted Baby Potatoes with Dill

2 pounds baby potatoes

2 tablespoons olive oil

½ teaspoon sea salt

2 tablespoons chopped fresh dill, stems removed

Preheat oven to 400°. Place potatoes on a jelly roll pan and drizzle with olive oil. Sprinkle the sea salt and chopped dill evenly over the potatoes. Bake 30 minutes or until the potatoes begin to brown. Serves 8.

Very Veggie Puree

3 pounds carrots, chunked (approximately 8 large)

2 medium turnips, peeled and chunked

1 onion, chopped

1 head garlic, cloves peeled and crushed

8 cups celery root

½ teaspoon marjoram

½ teaspoon celery salt

2 bay leaves

15 green peppercorns, crushed

1 teaspoon sea salt

8 cups water

Place all vegetables and spices in a large stock pot,; pour water over vegetable mixture. Cook on medium-high heat and bring to a boil; stirring occasionally. Reduce heat and simmer for 30-40 minutes or until vegetables are cooked through and soft but not mushy. Remove cooked vegetables from the pot with a slotted spoon and set aside. Remove the bay leaves and discard. Remove 2 cups broth and set aside. Place medium portions of the vegetables in a blender and pour in enough broth to just cover. Pulse on puree until the mixture is smooth. Continue the process until all the vegetables and all but the 2 cups of reserved broth is used. Use the puree as a side dish, base for grilled meats or in Very Veggie Soup, See Soups & Stews, page 107. Makes approximately 10 cups.

Cinnamon Fried Apples & Sweet Potatoes

3 (15-ounce) cans cooked, unsweetened sweet potatoes, cut into small pieces

1 large sweet apple, peeled, cored and sliced

1 large tart apple, peeled, cored and sliced

¾ teaspoon freshly grated nutmeg, divided (or 1 teaspoon dried and divided)

¾ teaspoon cardamom powder, divided

1 teaspoon cinnamon, divided

½ cup agave nectar

Place sweet potato pieces in a 9-by-13-inch glass baking dish and set aside. Preheat oven to 375°. Place apple slices in a small skillet and cook about 3 minutes on medium heat. Stir in ½ teaspoon of the freshly grated nutmeg and ½ teaspoon of the cardamom. Continue cooking for another 2-3 minutes. Sprinkle the apple slices with ½ teaspoon cinnamon and continue cooking until the apple slices are a bit brown and tender. Remove from heat and set aside. Sprinkle the sweet potatoes with the remaining nutmeg, cardamom and cinnamon and stir in the agave nectar. Gently fold the apples into the sweet potato mixture and bake uncovered for 20-25 minutes. Serves 8.

Roasted Root Veggies

12 whole carrots with green, trimmed

3 large potatoes, well scrubbed and cut into evenly sized pieces

2 turnips, peeled and cut into evenly sized pieces

2 yellow onions, peeled and cut into medium-sized pieces

3 tablespoons chopped garlic

⅓ cup olive oil

2 large sprigs fresh dill, stems removed

Preheat oven to 450°. Place all vegetables on a shallow baking pan evenly in a single layer. Sprinkle vegetables evenly with the chopped garlic, then evenly distribute olive oil over vegetables. Tear the dill fronds into pieces and place pieces intermittently with vegetables. Place in oven and roast for 15-20 minutes or until vegetables are fork tender. Serves 6.

Cranberry-Glazed Sweet Potatoes

1½ pounds cubed, cooked sweet potatoes

1 (16-ounce) can gelled cranberry sauce

¼ cup turbinado sugar

⅓ cup orange juice

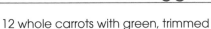 2 tablespoons clarified butter

Preheat oven to 350°. Place the cooked sweet potatoes in a 2-quart casserole and set aside. Place the cranberry sauce and raw sugar in a small saucepan. Stir until combined and then cook over medium heat, stirring often until the sugar dissolves. Stir in the orange juice and the butter and continue cooking until sauce is heated through. Pour cranberry mixture over the sweet potatoes evenly and bake uncovered for 20-25 minutes. Serves 6.

Spicy Summer Squash

1 teaspoon chipotle olive oil

3 cups cubed summer squash

1 medium onion, chopped

¼ teaspoon sea salt

2 tablespoons chopped green chilies

Heat olive oil in a 10-inch skillet over medium heat. Add summer squash and onion and cook until the onion appears translucent. Stir in the sea salt and green chilies. Continue cooking until the squash is fork tender. Serves 6.

Peppered Parsnips

2 tablespoons clarified butter

4 medium parsnips, thinly sliced

2 large red bell peppers, thinly sliced

3 cloves chopped garlic

½ teaspoon green peppercorns, crushed

¼ teaspoon freshly ground black pepper

½ teaspoon sea salt

Melt the clarified butter in a 10-inch skillet; add the parsnips and cook over medium heat for 5-6 minutes. Add the red bell peppers and the garlic; cook for 2-3 minutes longer. Stir in the crushed peppercorns, black pepper and sea salt. Continue cooking 4-6 minutes until vegetables are tender. Serves 4.

Orange Carrots & Celery

2 tablespoons clarified butter

3 cups thinly sliced carrots

2 cups thinly sliced celery

½ cup orange juice

½ teaspoon sea salt

Melt the clarified butter in a 12-inch skillet, then stir in the carrots. Cook over medium heat for 3-4 minutes then add the celery. Cook for 2-3 minutes longer; add orange juice and sea salt and bring to a boil. Reduce heat; simmer until orange juice is absorbed by the vegetables. Serves 6.

Nutrition Tip! One cup cooked beans has more potassium than a banana.

Easy Fennel Gratin

        4 cups water

        2 large fennel bulbs, trimmed and cut into evenly sized wedges

        2 teaspoons olive oil

        ¼ cup vegan Parmesan

        ¼ teaspoon sea salt

        ⅛ teaspoon black pepper

Bring the water to a boil in a medium sauce pan. Add the fennel wedges and cook for 5-6 minutes. Drain well and place fennel wedges in a 3-quart baking dish. Drizzle the fennel with olive oil, then sprinkle the vegan Parmesan over the fennel evenly. Season with the sea salt and black pepper; bake 15-20 minutes until lightly golden brown. Serves 4.

Quinoa Stuffed Tomatoes

        6 large heirloom tomatoes

        1 cup coarsely chopped onion

        1 teaspoon olive oil

        1 tablespoon chopped garlic

        1½ teaspoons thyme

         teaspoon sea salt

        ⅛ teaspoon black pepper

        1½ cups cooked quinoa

        ½ cup cooked white beans, mashed

        3 teaspoons vegan Parmesan

Preheat oven to 375°. Slice the tops off tomatoes and remove and discard the middle part of the core; set tops aside. Remove insides of tomatoes discarding the seeds and preserving the fleshy part, being careful not to tear the outer flesh, and set aside. Chop the tomato tops and the fleshy insides and set aside. Place the chopped onion, olive oil, chopped garlic and spices in a large mixing bowl. Stir mixture to combine. Add the quinoa and white beans, then add the chopped tomatoes and mix well. Place an equal amount of the stuffing mixture into each of the tomatoes and place them in a shallow 8-by-8-inch baking dish. Sprinkle the top of each tomato with the dairy-free Parmesan and bake for 15-20 minutes until heated thoroughly and golden brown. Serves 6.

Glazed Sweet Potatoes & Pineapple

        2 (15-ounce) cans sweet potatoes (no sugar added or without syrup)

        1 (20-ounce) can pineapple in its own juice, drained, with juice reserved

        ¾ cup sucanat

        3 tablespoons potato starch flour

        ⅓ cup maple syrup

 2 tablespoons clarified butter
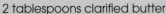

Preheat oven to 350°. Place sweet potatoes and pineapple in a 2-quart baking dish and set aside. Place reserved pineapple juice and sucanat in a saucepan and cook over medium heat until it begins to boil. Sprinkle in the potato starch flour while stirring constantly; reduce heat and stir in maple syrup. Continue to cook on low until thickened.

Stir in the clarified butter and set aside. Pour the glaze evenly over the potatoes and pineapple. Place in oven and bake for 30 minutes until heated through and bubbly. Serves 8.

$\mathcal{J}$weet Potato Casserole

3 cups cooked, mashed sweet potatoes
1 cup sucanat, divided
2 eggs, lightly beaten
½ teaspoon sea salt
½ cup vanilla soy milk
1 teaspoon vanilla
 ½ cup clarified butter, melted and divided
1 teaspoon molasses
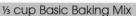 ⅓ cup Basic Baking Mix
1 cup coarsely chopped pecans

Preheat oven to 350°. In a mixing bowl combine the mashed sweet potatoes, ½ cup of the sucanat, beaten eggs, sea salt, soy milk, vanilla and ¼ cup of the melted, clarified butter. Stir the mixture until smooth, then pour evenly into a buttered 1½-quart baking dish; set aside. In another mixing bowl combine the remaining sucanat and remaining clarified butter. Cream until blended. Add the molasses; gently fold in baking mix and pecans. Pour the pecan mixture evenly over the top of the sweet potato mixture. Bake 35 minutes or until completely set in the middle. Serves 6.

$\mathcal{J}$weet Potato & Apple Stuffing

1 pound sweet potatoes, peeled, cubed and cooked until tender, but still firm
¾ cup chopped onion
¼ cup chopped celery
½ teaspoon sea salt
¼ teaspoon black pepper
½ cup natural apple juice, divided
1 cup chopped tart apples
⅛ teaspoon cinnamon
⅛ teaspoon freshly grated nutmeg
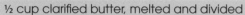 ⅛ teaspoon ground cloves
1 cup soft Sami's Millet & Flax Bread crumbs
3 tablespoon clarified butter, melted

Preheat oven to 350°. Place sweet potatoes in a large mixing bowl; set aside. Place the onion, celery, sea salt and black pepper in a skillet over medium heat and cook for 1-2 minutes just to soften the vegetables. Pour in ¼ cup of the apple juice and continue to cook for another 2-3 minutes. Add the chopped apples, cinnamon, nutmeg and ground cloves and continue to cook until the vegetables and apples are tender, but still firm. Add the vegetable mixture to the sweet potatoes and stir to combine. Stir in the soft bread crumbs, the remaining apple juice and the melted, clarified butter. Place stuffing mixture into a 9-by-13-inch buttered baking dish and bake for 30 minutes or until heated through and lightly brown. Serves 6.

Side & Salads

Wesley Hapner in the kitchen stir frying

Lemon Dill Potato Salad

    4 pounds red potatoes
    ½ of a sweet onion, chopped
    6 celery ribs, chopped
    ¼ cup olive oil
    ¼ cup canola oil
    1 lemon, juiced
    ½ tablespoon dill weed
    ¼ teaspoon sea salt
    1½ teaspoons chopped garlic

Cut potatoes into bite-sizes pieces but do not peel. Boil red potatoes until fork tender. Drain and cover with ice or ice water for 15 minutes and then drain again. Put potatoes in a medium-sized mixing bowl and add onion and celery; stir to mix. In another bowl, mix oils and lemon juice; add spices and garlic. Mix well; pour over potato mixture and chill for at least 1 hour before serving. Serves 8-10.

Grilled Tofu

    1 package extra firm water packed tofu
    ¾ tablespoon fresh ginger root, chopped
    1 tablespoon toasted sesame oil
    ¼ cup sucanat
    ½ cup orange juice
    ¾ cup wheat-free tamari
    ¼ cup white wine or apple juice

Slice tofu into 1½-inch cubes. Set aside. In a small bowl combine ginger root, sesame oil, sucanat, orange juice, tamari and wine (or apple juice). Mix well to combine. Add tofu to the mixture and cover the bowl. Marinate in the refrigerator for 1-2 hours. Skewer cubes of tofu and grill over direct heat for 5-6 minutes, turning once during grill time. Serves 4-6. Note: If using wooden skewers, make certain they have been soaked in water for at least 1 hour before use.

French Herbed Rice

    1 cup jasmine rice
    1 cup brown rice
    2½ cups water
    1 teaspoon olive oil
    ¼ teaspoon garlic powder
    1 teaspoon herbs de Provence

In a medium saucepan, combine jasmine and brown rice and water. Cook rice on medium heat until it begins to boil. Reduce heat, cover and simmer for 30-40 minutes until rice is tender. Stir in olive oil, garlic powder and herbs. Serves 8.

Cold Southwest Noodle Salad

2-3 ounces bean thread noodles, cooked

1 (14 ½ ounce) can black beans, rinsed and drained

1¼ cup carrots, sliced into ¼-inch coins

2 tablespoons green chilies

2 teaspoons minced garlic

½ cup canola oil

¼ cup red wine vinegar

3 tablespoons ketchup

2 tablespoons water

1 tablespoon agave nectar

2 tablespoons salsa

Place the bean thread noodles, black beans and carrots in a large bowl and set aside. Combine the green chilies, garlic, canola oil, red wine vinegar, ketchup, water, agave nectar and salsa in a blender. Pulse blender on puree 3-5 times, stirring occasionally. Continue to pulse on puree until the mixture is smooth. Stir the pureed mixture into the noodles and vegetables until blended. Chill for 30 minutes. Serves 4-6.

Carrot Coconut Salad

3 cups shredded carrots

1½ cups shredded coconut

1 cup raisins

½ cup canola mayonnaise

½ teaspoon cinnamon

1 tablespoon honey

In a 2-quart serving bowl combine the carrots, coconut and raisins. Stir ingredients until well blended; set aside. In a small mixing bowl combine the canola mayonnaise, cinnamon and honey and stir until the mixture is smooth. Pour the mayonnaise mixture over the carrot mixture and stir together until well coated. Chill for at least 1 hour before serving. Serves 10-12.

Dilled Mushroom Rice

2½ cups cooked rice (brown or white)

2 tablespoons vegetable broth

¼ cup canola mayonnaise

7 ounces sliced fresh mushrooms

½ teaspoon garlic salt

2 tablespoons freshly chopped dill or 1½ teaspoons dill weed

Preheat oven to 350°. Combine rice, vegetable broth and mayonnaise in a mixing bowl. Stir in the fresh mushrooms; add the garlic salt and dill. Stir ingredients to combine well. Pour mixture evenly into a buttered 9-by-9-inch glass casserole dish and bake for 25-30 minutes or until heated through and top is nicely browned. Serves 6.

Italian Vegetable Salad

1 cup green onion pieces (¾ to 1 inch in length)
1 ⅓ cup sliced celery
¼ cup mild pepper rings
1 red bell pepper, thinly sliced
1½ cups grape tomatoes, halved
⅓ cup sliced green olives

⅔ cup basil olive oil
20 green peppercorns, crushed
1 teaspoon Italian seasoning
⅓ cup balsamic vinegar

In a large bowl, combine green onions, celery, pepper rings, red bell pepper, grape tomato halves and green olive slices. Stir in the olive oil, crushed peppercorns and Italian seasoning to mix well. Pour balsamic vinegar over the top of vegetables and stir to combine mixture well. Refrigerate for at least 1 hour. Serves 10-12.

Gluten-Free Rolled Pierogies

3 cups Creamy Mashed Potatoes
½ cup Tofu Sour Cream
1 teaspoon garlic powder
10 green peppercorns, crushed
¼ teaspoon sea salt
1 cup soy mozzarella shreds
4 cups very warm water
36 tapioca sheets

In a large mixing bowl combine the mashed potatoes and sour cream. Stir in the garlic powder, crushed peppercorns, sea salt and soy shreds. Combine well. In a large bowl place the very warm water and 4 of the tapioca sheets. Soak the sheets until they are pliable; pat dry and lay on a flat work surface. Place 2 to 2½ tablespoons of the potato mixture about 1 inch from the edge of the circular sheet. Bring the 1-inch portion of the tapioca sheet over the potato mixture, fold in sides of tapioca sheet and roll to form a small egg roll shape. Continue soaking and filling process. Deep-fry potato rolls for 5-6 minutes at 375°. Makes approximately 36 pierogie rolls.

Lettuce Tip! Core a head of lettuce easily by gently pounding the head, core down on the counter; the core will pull out effortlessly.

Sweet Potato Salad

3 medium sweet potatoes, peeled and cubed

2 tablespoons sliced ginger root

2 tablespoons fresh lemon juice

1 cup canola mayonnaise

2 tablespoons orange juice

2 tablespoons maple syrup

⅛ teaspoon sea salt

¼ teaspoon cinnamon

½ teaspoon freshly grated nutmeg

2 (6-ounce) cans mandarin oranges, well drained

1 small sweet apple cored, peeled and chopped

½ cup chopped pecans

In a 4-quart sauce pan bring sweet potatoes and ginger root to a boil and cook for 9 minutes or until sweet potatoes are cooked but firm. Drain potatoes thoroughly and remove ginger root slices. Toss sweet potatoes with the lemon juice to cover and set aside. In a small mixing bowl combine the canola mayonnaise, orange juice, maple syrup, sea salt, cinnamon and nutmeg. Stir well to incorporate ingredients; set aside. Place the mandarin oranges, chopped apple and pecans with the sweet potatoes and stir gently to combine. Slowly pour mayonnaise mixture over the sweet potato mixture and stir well to coat. Refrigerate for at least 1 hour and stir once before serving. Serves 6.

Mediterranean Tomato Salad

3 medium tomatoes, thinly sliced

¼ cup olive oil

3 tablespoons freshly chopped basil

¼ cup mixed Greek olives, sliced

½ teaspoon garlic powder

¼ teaspoon sea salt

1 teaspoon garlic pepper

1 tablespoon vegan Parmesan (optional)

Place tomatoes in a glass bowl. Pour olive oil over tomatoes. Top the tomato mixture with the chopped basil and sliced Greek olives. Stir lightly to combine. Add garlic powder, sea salt and garlic pepper. Mix well. Cover and place in the refrigerator for at least 1 hour; sprinkle with vegan Parmesan just before serving (if desired). Serves 4.

Risotto Milanese

2 tablespoons clarified butter

1 sweet onion, finely chopped

1½ cups Arborio rice

½ cup white wine

4-5 cups warm chicken broth

1 pinch of crushed saffron

1 cup vegan Parmesan

2 tablespoon freshly chopped parsley

Sea salt and black pepper to taste

In a 3-quart sauce pan melt clarified butter over medium heat. Add the chopped sweet onion and sauté until translucent. Stir in the Arborio rice and toast for about 1 minute, stirring constantly. Add the white wine and reduce until all the liquid is absorbed. Add 1 cup of the warm chicken broth and reduce the mixture while continually stirring until all the liquid is absorbed. Continue this step until the rice is creamy and not at all grainy. If all the chicken broth is used and the rice is still not without grain, add ½ cup water and reduce it again. Remove from heat and stir in the crushed saffron and Parmesan. Stir in the fresh parsley and serve immediately. Serves 6.

Twice Baked Potato Casserole

6 medium potatoes, baked, cooled and cubed

¼ teaspoon sea salt, divided

¼ teaspoon black pepper, divided

1 pound natural turkey bacon, cooked and chopped

3 cups Tofu Sour Cream, divided

2 tablespoons vegan Parmesan, divided

1½ cup soy mozzarella shreds

1½ cups soy cheddar shreds

4 scallions, chopped

Preheat oven to 350°. In a 9-by-13-inch baking dish, place ½ of the potatoes in an even layer. Sprinkle potatoes with ⅛ teaspoon of the sea salt and ⅛ teaspoon of the black pepper. Layer ½ of the turkey bacon over the potato mixture and then spread 1½ cups of the sour cream over the top. Sprinkle with 1 tablespoon of the dairy-free Parmesan and then top with ¾ cup of the soy mozzarella and the soy cheddar shreds. Repeat the complete process and top with the chopped scallions. Bake for 20-25 minutes or until heated through and golden brown. Serves 10-12.

Gluten-Free Onion Rings

Canola oil for frying

1 cup sorghum flour

½ cup brown rice flour

½ cup white rice flour

2 teaspoons corn-free baking powder

½ teaspoon sea salt

1 cup plus 2 tablespoons soy milk

2 teaspoons olive oil

4 beaten eggs

3-4 large sweet onions sliced into ¼-inch thick slices and separated into rings.

Preheat cooking oil to 375°. In a large mixing bowl combine the sorghum, brown rice and white rice flours and stir to combine. Add the baking powder and sea salt; slowly stir in the soy milk, olive oil and beaten eggs. Stir the mixture until mixed well. With a pair of tongs, gently dip the onion rings into the batter to coat completely. Allow excess to drip off the onion when removing from the batter and place on a tray in a single layer. Place in the hot oil and fry the rings for about 3 minutes, turning once after 1½ minutes of cooking. Drain on a thick layer of paper towels; serve immediately. Serves 8.

Rice Bread Stuffing

4 ½ cups Sami's Millet & Flax toasted bread cubes

¾ cup chopped celery

½ cup chopped onion

¼ teaspoon thyme

½ teaspoon sea salt

½ teaspoon sage

¼ teaspoon black pepper

 6 tablespoons clarified butter, melted

½ to ¾ cups vegetable or chicken broth

Preheat oven to 350°. In a large mixing bowl combine the bread cubes, celery, onion and spices. Stir gently to combine. Pour the melted clarified butter over the mixture and then gently stir in the broth ¼ cup at a time to acquire the moistness desired. Place in a shallow baking dish and bake for 20-25 minutes or until golden brown on top. Serves 6.

Gluten-Free Vegetable Stuffing

4½ cups Sami's Millet & Flax toasted bread cubes

6 celery ribs, diced

1 cup diced carrots

2 small onions, diced

4 ounces fresh mushrooms, chopped

½ teaspoon garlic powder

½ teaspoon sea salt

¼ teaspoon thyme

¼ teaspoon sage

⅛ teaspoon black pepper

6 tablespoons clarified butter, melted

½ cup vegetable broth

Preheat oven to 350°. Place the bread cubes in a large mixing bowl; set aside. In a medium skillet over medium heat sauté celery, carrots, onions and mushrooms until all the vegetables are tender. Stir in the spices and remove from heat. Pour the vegetable mixture over the bread cubes and stir to combine. Pour the clarified butter over the mixture and stir in the broth until well combined. Place in a 9-by-13-inch baking dish and bake for 20-25 minutes. Serves 8.

Tip! Romaine lettuce stays fresher longer if washed, dried, wrapped in a layer of paper toweling and refrigerated in a resealable bag.

Flavor Tip! Spice up a green salad by adding different fresh herbs.

Grandma Frank's Lettuce Salad

- ½ head iceberg lettuce, chopped
- 2 hard-boiled eggs
- 4 tablespoons Grandma's Mayonnaise Dressing (See Sauces & Such, page 104)

Place lettuce in even amounts in 4 salad bowls. Chop ½ a hard-boiled egg on top of each amount of lettuce. Place 1 tablespoon of dressing atop lettuce mixture. Serve. Serves 4.

Mom's Three-Bean Salad

- 1 (8-ounce) can cut yellow wax beans, drained
- 1 (8-ounce) can cut green beans, drained
- 1 (8-ounce) can red kidney beans, rinsed and drained
- ½ cup chopped onion
- ½ cup chopped green pepper
- ¼ cup canola oil
- ½ cup apple cider vinegar
- 3 tablespoons ground sucanat
- 1 teaspoon celery seed
- 1 clove garlic, minced

In a large bowl combine the wax, green and kidney beans with the onion and green pepper; set aside. In a screw-top jar combine the apple cider vinegar, canola oil, ground sucanat, celery seed and garlic. Cover tightly and shake vigorously. Pour the dressing over the vegetable mixture and stir lightly to coat completely. Cover bowl and refrigerate for at least 4 hours, stirring often. Serves 6.

Marinated Tomato Salad

- 6 cups grape tomatoes, cut into halves
- 2 tablespoons olive oil
- 1 tablespoon Dijon mustard
- 2 tablespoons chopped garlic
- ½ teaspoon freshly ground black pepper
- ½ teaspoon sea salt
- 1 tablespoon chopped, fresh oregano

Place tomatoes in a serving bowl; set aside. In a small bowl, whisk together olive oil and Dijon mustard. Stir in garlic, sea salt, black pepper and fresh oregano. Pour dressing mixture over the tomatoes and stir to coat completely. Cover and refrigerate for at least 6 hours before serving. Serves 6

Sides & **Salads** 93

ell Pepper Potato Salad

6 medium potatoes, cooked and cut into even chunks

1¼ cup chopped, mixed red and yellow bell pepper

½ cup chopped onion

¾ cup canola mayonnaise

1½ tablespoons mustard

⅛ teaspoon sea salt

1½ teaspoons freshly chopped parsley

2 teaspoons fresh chives

In a mixing bowl combine the potatoes, bell peppers and onions; set aside. In a small mixing bowl mix the mayonnaise and mustard, stir in the sea salt, parsley and chives and stir until combined. Pour the dressing mixture over potato mixture and stir to coat completely. Chill; serve. Serves 8.

andarin Crab Meat Salad

1½ cups flaked crab meat

4 tablespoons canola mayonnaise

1 (11-ounce) can mandarin oranges, drained

⅔ cup roasted red bell peppers, diced

½ teaspoon cayenne pepper

4 tablespoons chopped chives, divided

4 cups mixed fresh greens

Place the crab meat in a mixing bowl and add the mayonnaise; stir to combine. Gently stir in the mandarin oranges, roasted red peppers, cayenne pepper and 2 tablespoon of the chives. Mix gently until all ingredients are well combined; set aside. Evenly distribute the mixed greens onto 4 salad plates. Top the greens with equal portions of the crab mixture and sprinkle some of the remaining chives atop each salad. Serve immediately. Serves 4.

resh Fennel Orange Salad

1 large fennel bulb, trimmed and thinly sliced

2 medium oranges peeled, seeded, sliced and broken into sections, membranes removed

1 tablespoon olive oil

1 tablespoon red wine vinegar

⅛ teaspoon sea salt

¼ teaspoon black pepper

2 tablespoons chopped dried cranberries

Place the fennel and orange sections in a large bowl; set aside. In a small mixing bowl whisk together the olive oil, red wine vinegar, sea salt and black pepper. Pour the dressing mixture over the fennel and orange mixture and stir to coat completely. Sprinkle the dried cranberries on top of the salad; chill and serve. Serves 6.

Fennel Radish Salad

1 bunch radishes, thinly sliced

1 fennel bulb, trimmed and thinly sliced

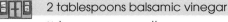
2 tablespoons olive oil

2 tablespoons balsamic vinegar

⅛ teaspoon sea salt

⅛ teaspoon black pepper

In a serving bowl combine the radishes and fennel; set aside. In a small mixing bowl whisk together the olive oil, balsamic vinegar, sea salt and pepper. Pour the dressing mixture over the vegetable mixture and stir to coat evenly. Chill for at least 30 minutes. Serves 6.

Southwest Vegetable Salad

1 red bell pepper, thinly sliced

4 baby cucumbers, thinly sliced

1 cup chunked baby carrots

½ medium red onion, chopped

1 (14½ ounce) can black beans, rinsed and drained

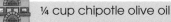
¼ cup chipotle olive oil

¼ cup sherry wine vinegar

2 tablespoons canola oil

2 cloves garlic

¼ teaspoon cumin

¼ teaspoon Ancho Chili Seasoning (See Sauces & Such, page 106)

⅛ teaspoon chili powder

⅛ teaspoon sea salt

½ teaspoon agave nectar

1 tablespoon parsley flakes

Place the red bell pepper, cucumbers, carrots, red onion and black beans in a 3-quart glass bowl. Stir to mix the vegetables; set aside. In a blender or food processor combine the chipotle olive oil, sherry wine vinegar, canola oil and garlic. Puree on pulse 2 or 3 times to chop the garlic. Add the cumin, ancho chili seasoning, chili powder, sea salt and agave nectar and puree again until completely blended. Stir parsley into vegetable mixture and then pour the dressing mixture over the vegetables. Stir to coat completely. Refrigerate for 1 hour before serving, stirring once or twice. Serves 8.

Skillet Quinoa

1 teaspoon olive oil
1½ cups chopped onion
1 tablespoon chopped garlic
1 teaspoon sea salt
4 cups cooked quinoa
½ cup vegan Parmesan
1 tablespoon parsley flakes

Place the olive oil, onion and garlic in a large skillet over medium heat. Saute vegetables until onion is translucent. Stir in sea salt and cooked quinoa. Continue to cook until the quinoa begins to brown. Stir in vegan Parmesan and parsley flakes. Serves 8.

Marinated Asparagus Salad

1 pound fresh asparagus spears, trimmed
2 tablespoons rice vinegar
4 tablespoons wheat-free tamari
2 teaspoons canola oil
4 teaspoons turbinado sugar
½ teaspoon toasted sesame oil
¼ cup toasted pecans

Cook asparagus in salted boiling water until it is tender but crisp. Drain; rinse in cold water; set aside. In a gallon resealable bag, mix rice vinegar, tamari, canola oil, sugar and sesame oil. Place asparagus spears in the bag, crush bag over asparagus to coat with vinegar mixture. Place in refrigerator and marinate overnight, turning once or twice to ensure all spears are coated. Remove asparagus spears from bag; place on serving plate and top with toasted pecans. This may be served with a small amount of marinade for dressing as well. Serves 4.

Quick & Easy Spicy Thai Pasta

½ cup soy nut butter

2 tablespoons very hot water

2 cups brown rice pasta; cooked but firm

2 tablespoons wheat-free tamari

3-4 drops hot pepper sauce

⅛ teaspoon coriander

In a small bowl combine soy nut butter and hot water; set aside. Place cooked pasta in a skillet over low heat. Stir in the soy nut butter mixture and tamari. Add hot pepper sauce and coriander and stir well to combine. Serve immediately. Makes 2 main dish portions or 4 side dish portions.

Sandy Spaghetti

4 cups rice spaghetti, cooked but firm

4 tablespoons olive oil

1 tablespoon minced garlic

½ teaspoon red pepper flakes

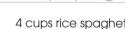
1½ cups Sami's Millet & Flax dry breadcrumbs, coarsely ground

Place spaghetti in a serving bowl; set aside. Pour olive oil in a skillet over medium heat. Stir in garlic and cook to brown slightly. Add red pepper flakes and stir in breadcrumbs. Cook for 1-2 minutes to brown mixture slightly. Pour crumb mixture over spaghetti and stir well to combine. Serves 4.

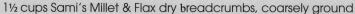

Taco Salad

1 pound lean beef strips

1 tablespoon Taco Seasoning (See Sauces & Such, page 106)

6 cups torn romaine lettuce leaves

1 cup chopped tomatoes

½ cup chopped onion

1 cup salsa

½ cup Tofu Sour Cream

Place beef strips in a skillet over medium heat and cook for 2-3 minutes. Stir in seasoning mix and cook another 3 minutes until beef strips are fully cooked; set aside. On four separate dinner plates, place 1½ cups romaine leaves. Top each lettuce portion with ¼ cup tomatoes, 2 tablespoons onion, ¼ cup salsa and 2 tablespoons sour cream. Serve with Tapioca Chips if desired. See Breads, Muffins & Crackers, page 45. Serves 4.

Tip! Cook extra bacon ahead; crumble and keep in the freezer to use in recipes or for salads, casseroles or toppings.

Tomato Quinoa Pilaf

1 cup quinoa

2 cups tomato juice

2 tablespoons clarified butter

½ teaspoon sea salt

½ cup chopped tomatoes

Rinse quinoa thoroughly under cold running water; drain. In a medium sauce pan combine quinoa and tomato juice; bring to a boil. Reduce heat to medium low; cover; cook 12-15 minutes or until the liquid is absorbed and the quinoa looks transparent. Stir in clarified butter and sea salt; transfer to a serving bowl and top with chopped tomatoes. Serves 4.

Strawberry Romaine Salad

4 cups torn romaine leaves

1 cup sliced strawberries

1 sweet onion, thinly sliced into rings

4 teaspoons pine nuts

Place 1 cup romaine leaves and ¼ cup strawberries in four separate salad bowls or plates. Top with 3-4 onion rings and 1 teaspoon pine nuts. Serve with Fresh Strawberry Vinaigrette. See Sauces & Such, page 105. Serves 4.

Artichoke Aioli, **page 105**

Zucchini Relish

    8 cups zucchini squash, grated
    4 cups white onion, chopped
    5 tablespoons sea salt
    2¼ cups apple cider vinegar
    5 cups sucanat
    2 tablespoons chopped red bell pepper
    2 tablespoons celery seed
    ½ teaspoon pickling spice
    1 teaspoon nutmeg
    1 teaspoon turmeric
    1 teaspoon dry mustard

Place zucchini, onion and sea salt in a large mixing bowl; cover with water and soak overnight. Drain mixture and rinse well with cold water and drain again. In a medium saucepan combine vinegar and sucanat; bring to a boil. Remove from heat and stir in red bell pepper, celery seed, pickling spice, nutmeg, turmeric and dry mustard. Pour liquid over zucchini and onion mixture and stir to combine. Pack in 6 pint jars that have been heated and sterilized in a dishwasher, and process in a hot water bath for 10 minutes. Makes 6 pints.

Tartar Sauce

    1 cup canola mayonnaise
    2 tablespoons Zucchini Relish (recipe above)
    ⅛ teaspoon sea salt

In a small bowl, combine canola mayonnaise and relish. Stir until well combined then add sea salt until well-combined and serve. Makes 1 cup.

Teriyaki Sauce

    1¼ cups wheat-free tamari
    ¾ cup honey
    ¼ cup water
    ⅓ cup blush wine or 100% apple juice
    2 tablespoons minced garlic

Combine all ingredients until honey is completely incorporated. Use for stir-fry or as a marinade. Makes approximately 2½ cups.

*P*izza Sauce

1 (6-ounce) can tomato paste

1 (8-ounce) can tomato sauce

¼ cup water

4 tablespoons olive oil

1 teaspoon oregano

½ teaspoon thyme

½ teaspoon crushed rosemary

½ teaspoon basil

⅛ teaspoon sea salt

⅛ teaspoon pepper

Mix all ingredients together in a saucepan and simmer for 20-25 minutes. Makes approximately 1 cup.

*T*ofu Mayonnaise

1 (8-ounce) package silken tofu

2 tablespoons canola oil

3 tablespoons fresh lemon juice

¾ teaspoon sea salt

Put tofu, including liquid, into a blender. Pulse blender on purée until smooth. Add canola oil and lemon juice and pulse again to blend. Add salt and purée until mixture is smooth. Makes 1 cup.

Tip! An easy way to store fresh ginger is to peel the entire root, place it in a resealable bag and freeze for up to three months. To use, remove and grate amount specified when needed.

Poppy Seed Dressing

½ cup olive oil

6 tablespoons apple cider vinegar

¾ cup organic sugar

1 small white onion, quartered

½ teaspoon dry mustard

¼ teaspoon sea salt

⅛ teaspoon pepper

1 teaspoon poppy seeds

In a blender combine olive oil, apple cider vinegar and sugar. On medium speed, pulse several times to combine ingredients. Add onion and continue to pulse until onion is pureed. Add dry mustard, sea salt and pepper; pulse again until ingredients are well combined. Pour dressing into bowl and stir in poppy seeds. Makes approximately 1 cup.

Honey Mustard Salad Dressing

½ cup stone ground mustard

4 tablespoons honey

¼ teaspoon pepper

⅛ teaspoon sea salt

In a small bowl combine the mustard and honey. Mix them until they are blended. Add pepper and sea salt; stir until combined. Serve on any green or mixed salad. Makes approximately ¾ cup.

Honey Mustard Glaze

⅓ cup honey

4 tablespoons spicy brown mustard

2 tablespoons water

⅛ teaspoon sea salt

In a small bowl combine the honey and the mustard. Add water and sea salt; stir until well combined. Use on pork or chicken. Can be stored in refrigerator for 7-10 days in an airtight container. Makes approximately 1 cup.

Tip! Don't keep seasonings in the cabinet above the stove top. Exposure to heat causes spices to lose flavor.

Confetti Salsa

1¼ cup chopped onion
1 large yellow tomato, chopped
1 large red tomato, chopped
1 jalapeno pepper, seeded and diced
1½ cup chopped green bell pepper
1 tablespoon chopped garlic
2 tablespoons red wine vinegar
½ teaspoon cilantro
1 tablespoon parsley
1 teaspoon basil

In a mixing bowl combine the onion, tomatoes, jalapeno, green pepper and garlic. Mix well. Stir in red wine vinegar, cilantro, parsley and basil. Place in a covered container and chill until ready to serve. Makes approximately 4 cups.

Pineapple & Ginger Salsa

2 cups fresh pineapple cut into small pieces
1 cup peeled, seeded and chopped tomato
4 green onions, sliced
1 jalapeno pepper, seeded and chopped
2 tablespoons red wine vinegar
3 cloves garlic, chopped
2 teaspoons toasted sesame oil
1½ teaspoons honey
2 teaspoons freshly grated ginger
½ teaspoon sea salt
¼ cup pineapple juice

In a small bowl combine the pineapple, tomato, green onions, jalapeno pepper and stir. Add the red wine vinegar, garlic, toasted sesame oil, honey, grated ginger and sea salt. Stir in the pineapple juice until well combined. Refrigerate before serving. This salsa is terrific when served with the Salmon Kabobs, page 76. Makes approximately 3½ cups.

Turkey Pasta Sauce

7 ounces mushrooms, halved
1 teaspoon minced garlic
1 quart Seasoned Tomato Sauce
⅛ teaspoon sea salt
2 cups cooked turkey breast

Place the mushrooms and minced garlic in a 3-quart saucepan,; stir in the tomato sauce, sea salt and turkey breast. Cook on medium heat, stirring often until the mixture is heated through. Serve over whole soybean or rice pasta. Makes approximately 1 ½ quarts.

Red Raspberry Freezer Jam

  2 cups crushed red raspberries
  3 cups turbinado sugar
  1½ tablespoons lemon juice
  3 ounces liquid pectin

In a large bowl, stir together the crushed berries and turbinado sugar. Continue stirring for 10 minutes to help dissolve the sugar. It is OK if there are still some sugar crystals. Stir in the lemon juice and liquid pectin and continue stirring another 4 minutes. Immediately pour berry mixture into prepared jars leaving ½-inch head space for freezer expansion. Seal jars; leave jam set at room temperature for 24 hours. It may be used and refrigerated immediately or frozen for up to 9 months. Makes approximately 3 cups.

Sweet Spicy Mustard Dressing

  2 tablespoons yellow mustard
  ¼ teaspoon cayenne pepper
  2 tablespoons Tofu Sour Cream
  3 tablespoons soy milk
  2 tablespoons honey

Combine all ingredients until smooth and serve over a mixed green salad. Makes approximately ½ cup.

Sun-Dried Tomato Pesto

  ¾ cup chopped sun-dried tomatoes
  2 cloves garlic
  ½ cup plus 2 tablespoons basil olive oil
  ¼ cup chopped roasted red peppers
  ¼ cup freeze dried basil leaves
  ½ cup vegan Parmesan

Place the sun dried tomatoes and garlic in a blender and pour in the olive oil; pulse once or twice on puree. Add the roasted red peppers, basil leaves and vegan Parmesan. Continue to pulse until the mixture is smooth and completely blended. Makes approximately 2¼ cups.

Grandma's Mayonnaise Dressing

  1 cup canola mayonnaise
  2 teaspoons apple cider vinegar
  ¼ cup agave nectar
  2 tablespoons soy milk
  Sea salt and black pepper to taste

In a small bowl combine the mayonnaise, and apple cider vinegar. Whisk until smooth; add the agave nectar and soy milk. Continue to whisk until the mixture is smooth and creamy. Add the sea salt and black pepper. Serve over lettuce, cabbage or with raw vegetables. Makes approximately 1½ cups.

Fresh Basil Pesto

2 cups fresh basil leaves, packed
⅓ cup pine nuts
3 garlic cloves, minced
½ cup olive oil
½ cup vegan Parmesan
⅛ teaspoon sea salt
⅛ teaspoon black pepper

Place the basil leaves and pine nuts in a food processor. Pulse a few times to chop the leaves and the pine nuts. Add the garlic and pulse a few more times to blend. Slowly pour in the olive oil and pulse again to blend. Add the vegan Parmesan, sea salt and pepper and continue to pulse until smooth. Makes approximately 2 cups.

Fresh Strawberry Vinaigrette

8-10 fresh strawberries, cleaned and trimmed
2 cloves garlic, sliced
⅓ cup strawberry balsamic vinegar
2 tablespoons water
¼ cup olive oil

Place the strawberries and garlic in a blender; pulse a few times to chop. Pour in the strawberry balsamic vinegar and pulse a few more times to blend. Add the water and the olive oil and continue to pulse until the mixture is smooth. Makes approximately 1½ cups.

Artichoke Aioli

6 ounces marinated artichoke hearts, drained; chopped
8 cloves garlic
1½ cups canola mayonnaise
1 tablespoon garlic chives

In a food processor combine the artichoke hearts and the garlic. Pulse several times until the mixture is completely pureed. Stir in the canola mayonnaise and then the garlic chives. Serve with grilled beef or chicken. Makes approximately 2 ½ cups.

Béarnaise Sauce

2 egg yolks, slightly beaten
2 tablespoons lemon juice
½ cup clarified butter, divided
1 tablespoon minced onion
1¼ teaspoons tarragon
2 tablespoons white wine

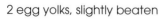

In small pan stir yolks and lemon juice briskly with wooden spoon. Stir in ¼ cup of the butter and all of the onion and tarragon over low heat until melted. Add the rest of the butter. Stir briskly until butter is melted. Melt butter slowly. Stir in wine. Makes approximately 1 cup.

Taco Seasoning

2 tablespoons chili powder

1 tablespoon + 2 teaspoons paprika

4½ teaspoons cumin

2½ teaspoons onion powder

½ teaspoon garlic powder

⅛ teaspoon cayenne pepper

Combine all ingredients and store in an airtight container. Makes approximately ¼ cup.

Ancho Chili Seasoning

2 tablespoons ancho chili powder

2 tablespoons chili powder

3 tablespoons paprika

8 teaspoons cumin

5 teaspoons onion powder

1 teaspoons garlic powder

Combine all ingredients and store in a spice container. Makes approximately ¾ cup.

Chipotle Chili Seasoning

2 tablespoons chipotle chili powder

2 tablespoons chili powder

3 tablespoons paprika

8 teaspoons cumin

5 teaspoons onion powder

1 teaspoons garlic powder

Combine all ingredients and store in a spice container. Makes approximately ¾ cup.

Butter Pecan Syrup

1 cup pecan pieces

¼ cup clarified butter, melted

1 ½ cup maple syrup

Place the pecans in a small bowl then stir in the melted, clarified butter and the maple syrup. Heat mixture in a small saucepan over low heat until heated through. Serve over pancakes. Makes approximately 2 cups.

Pantry Tip! When stocking your pantry, rotate items by the use or sell by dates so that items don't expire before you're able to use them.

Soups & Stews

Buffalo Chili, **page 110**

Chicken & Rice Stew

1 tablespoon clarified butter

½ tablespoon olive oil

2 boneless, skinless chicken breasts cut into small pieces

3 leeks, trimmed and sliced into strips, greens removed

2 tablespoons minced garlic

2 cups chopped carrots

1 green pepper, chopped

2½ (14½-ounce) cans chicken broth

5 cups water

⅓ cup brown rice

1½ teaspoons sea salt

½ teaspoon marjoram

1 teaspoon thyme

2 teaspoons parsley

Melt clarified butter and add olive oil in a large stockpot. Add chicken; cook for 3 minutes or until mostly white. Add leeks, garlic, carrots and green pepper. Sauté 3 minutes longer. Slowly add broth and water. Stir in brown rice; add herbs and spices. Bring to a boil; reduce heat and simmer for 1 hour. Serves 4-6.

Asian Vegetable Noodle Soup

1 tablespoon clarified butter

2 tablespoons olive oil

1 cup julienned, carrots

1 cup chopped celery

1 small onion, chopped

1 teaspoon sea salt

3 (14¼-ounce) cans vegetable broth

1 (14¼-ounce) can water

3 tablespoons wheat-free tamari

¾ tablespoon thyme

⅛ teaspoon cumin

¼ teaspoon Oriental five spice

4 cups cooked rice noodles, cooked and drained

1 (14½ ounce) can black beans, rinsed

In a medium sauté pan, melt clarified butter and mix with olive oil. Add carrots and sauté for 2-3 minutes. Add celery and onion and continue cooking until onion is translucent. Stir in sea salt; remove from heat and pour into stockpot. Add vegetable broth, water and tamari. Then add all herbs and spices. Simmer for 10 minutes. Add noodles and beans. Simmer another 20-25 minutes and serve. Serves 8. Note: Oriental five spice is a purchased blend.

urkey Rice Soup

1 onion, chopped

2 celery ribs, sliced

2 carrots, peeled and sliced into ¼-inch coins

10-12 fresh mushrooms, sliced

2 cups turkey breast, cooked and diced

4 cups turkey or chicken broth

2 (14¼-ounce) cans vegetable broth

1 teaspoon favorite salt-free blend

1 teaspoon parsley flakes

½ teaspoon thyme

¼ teaspoon basil

1 teaspoon sea salt

1 cup white rice

Place vegetables in a 6-quart stockpot and cook over medium heat for 3-5 minutes. Add turkey meat, all the broth and herbs, then rice. Bring to a boil; reduce to low heat and simmer for 45 minutes. Serves 8.

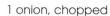imply Delicious Vegetarian Chili

1 tablespoon olive oil

2 onions, chopped

3 tablespoons minced garlic

1 jalapeno, seeded and chopped

1 green pepper, chopped

⅔ cup diced green chilies

½ tablespoon sea salt

½ tablespoon dry basil

1 tablespoon chili powder

2 bay leaves

1 (28-ounce) can diced tomatoes

1 (15-ounce) can tomato purée

1 (28-ounce) can crushed tomatoes

1 (14½-ounce) can diced fire-roasted tomatoes

2 (14½-ounce) cans hot water

2 cups textured soy protein, soaked in 3 cups water

2 (15½-ounce) cans pinto beans, rinsed and drained

In a large stock pot heat olive oil; add onion, garlic, jalapeno and green pepper. Sauté until onion is translucent. Add green chilies, sea salt, basil, chili powder and bay leaves; stir and cook for 2-3 minutes. Pour in diced, puréed, crushed and fire-roasted tomatoes. Add the cans of hot water and the textured soy protein. Stir well to blend; Add beans. Bring to a boil; reduce heat, cover and simmer for 45 minutes. Remove bay leaves before serving. Makes approximately 5 quarts.

Minestrone

2 tablespoons olive oil
1 pound lean ground beef or buffalo
1 medium onion, chopped
2 tablespoons chopped garlic
2 (14½-ounce) cans diced tomatoes
1 (14½-ounce) can vegetable broth
4 cups water
1 cup dry brown rice pasta
2 teaspoons Italian seasoning
½ teaspoon sea salt
1 (15-ounce) can cut green beans
1 (15-ounce) can pinto beans, rinsed and drained
1 (15-ounce) can garbanzo beans, rinsed and drained

In a medium skillet heat olive oil; add ground meat. Cook meat until it begins to brown. Add onion and garlic; cook 5-6 minutes longer. Place meat mixture in a 6-quart stockpot. Pour diced tomatoes, broth and water over meat. Bring mixture to a boil; add pasta, Italian seasoning and sea salt. Boil for 8-10 minutes or until pasta is tender. Add all beans; reduce heat and simmer for 10-15 minutes. Serves 10.

Buffalo Chili

1 tablespoon olive oil
2 pounds ground buffalo
1 medium onion, chopped
3½ tablespoons minced garlic
1 (4-ounce) can green chilies, chopped
2 (14½-ounce) cans diced tomatoes
1 (28-ounce) can crushed tomatoes
1 cup water
1 tablespoon sea salt
2 tablespoons chili powder
1 tablespoon cumin
1 (15½-ounce) can small white beans, rinsed and drained
1 (15½-ounce) can light red kidney beans, rinsed and drained

In a 6-quart stockpot heat olive oil; add buffalo and cook over medium heat until browned. Add onion; continue cooking until translucent. Add garlic and green chilies; cook 3-4 minutes longer. Add all tomatoes, water, sea salt and spices; stir in beans. Bring chili to a boil; reduce heat. Cover and simmer 45-60 minutes. Serves 12.

Split Pea & Ham Soup

1 tablespoon clarified butter
½ cup chopped onion
½ cup chopped carrots
1 (10-ounce) package dry split peas
4 cups chicken broth

3½ cups water

2 cups chopped, naturally smoked ham with no additives or preservatives

Sea salt and pepper to taste

In a large stockpot melt clarified butter and sauté onions and carrots until onion begins to soften. Add the dry split peas, chicken broth and water. Cook over medium heat for 45-60 minutes, stirring occasionally. Stir in the ham and cook for an additional 25-30 minutes or until thickened. Add sea salt and pepper to taste. Serves 8.

*I*talian Chicken Noodle Stew

- 1 tablespoon olive oil
- 4 boneless, skinless chicken breasts, split
- 2 tablespoons minced garlic
- ½ teaspoon Italian seasoning
- 2 (28-ounce) cans diced, fire-roasted tomatoes
- 4 cups cooked rice noodles

Pour olive oil in a small stockpot and heat on medium for about a minute. Place chicken portions in the oil and cook until the underside is brown. Turn the chicken portions and add the garlic. Cook about 2 minutes longer then sprinkle the Italian seasoning evenly over the chicken portions. Pour the fire-roasted tomatoes over the entire mixture and simmer until the chicken portions reach 180° on a meat thermometer. Stir in the rice noodles and serve. Serves 8.

*G*arlic Mashed Potato Soup

- 2 tablespoons clarified butter
- ½ cup Tofu Sour Cream
- 1 cup soy creamer
- 2 cups water
- 3 cups Creamy Mashed Potatoes
- 1 teaspoon sea salt
- 1 teaspoon garlic powder
- ½ teaspoon black pepper
- ⅓ cup potato flakes

In a 3-quart pan melt clarified butter over medium heat. Stir in the sour cream, soy creamer and water and stir until smooth. Gently stir in the mashed potatoes and continue to stir until mixture is smooth and creamy. Add the sea salt, garlic powder and black pepper, then stir in the potato flakes. Continue to cook until the soup is smooth and heated thoroughly. Serves 8.

Nutrition Tip! Eat beans. Beans contain ¼ of the USDA-recommended amount of protein for adults, and beans are low in fat.

Very Veggie Stew

4 cups potatoes

2 cups shredded red cabbage

4 cups chopped broccoli

4 cloves garlic, chopped

4 cups vegetable juice

4 cups Very Veggie Puree (See Vegetables, page 81)

2 cups water

½ teaspoon thyme

1 teaspoon favorite no-salt blend

2 cups chopped kale

Place potatoes, red cabbage, broccoli, garlic, vegetable juice, puree, water thyme and no-salt blend in a small stockpot. Bring mixture to a boil, reduce heat, cover and simmer for about 20 minutes. Stir in the chopped kale and simmer an additional 15 minutes or until vegetables are fork tender. Serves 12.

Potato, Pesto Pasta Soup

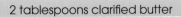

2 tablespoons clarified butter

¼ cup chopped sweet onion

2 tablespoons water

½ cup soy creamer

2 quarts plain soy milk

1 teaspoon sea salt

3 large potatoes, peeled, cooked and sliced

1½ cups cooked, shell-shaped rice pasta

1 cup Fresh Basil Pesto (See Sauces & Such, page 105)

In a 4-quart stockpot, over medium heat, melt the clarified butter. Add onion and cook until translucent. Stir in the water, soy creamer and soy milk. Add the sea salt, stir in the potatoes and the rice pasta. Continue to stir and cook for 1-2 minutes. Gently stir in the pesto and stir until completely blended and smooth. Cook an additional 3-4 minutes or until completely heated through. Serves 6.

Chicken Sausage Potato Soup

2 pounds chicken sausage

2 tablespoons chopped garlic

4 ribs celery, chopped

½ cup chopped onion

3½ cups water, divided

2 potatoes, peeled and chopped

3 tablespoons clarified butter

2 cups soy creamer

4 cups soy milk

1½ cups potato flakes

1 teaspoon sea salt

Place the chicken sausage and garlic n a large skillet. Cook on medium heat, until the sausage begins to change color. Add the celery and onion and cook the mixture until the sausage is completely cooked through and the vegetables are tender; set aside. Place 2 cups of the water in a 6-quart stockpot and bring to a boil; add the chopped potatoes and clarified butter. Cook for 10-12 minutes, stirring often until the potatoes are tender. Add the sausage mixture and stir to combine well. Stir in the soy creamer, soy milk and remaining water. Cook for another 2-3 minutes to heat through. Slowly stir in the potato flakes and sea salt. Continue to cook until the potato flakes are completely incorporated and the soup begins to thicken. Serves 12.

Beefy Black Bean Chili

⅓ cup chopped onion
1 pound browned beef steak pieces
1 (28-ounce) can diced fire-roasted tomatoes
1 (15-ounce) can diced tomatoes
2 (15-ounce) cans black beans, rinsed and drained
1 (15-ounce) can red chili beans
1 (4-ounce) can green chilies
½ teaspoon lime juice
3 cups vegetable juice
½ teaspoon hot pepper sauce
1½ cups water
2 teaspoons chili powder
¼ teaspoon sea salt
⅛ teaspoon pepper

Place the chopped onion, beef pieces, tomatoes, beans and green chilies in a large crockpot. Stir to blend. Add the lime and vegetable juice, hot pepper sauce and water. Stir in the chili powder, sea salt and pepper. Cook on low for 6 hours or on high for 3 hours. Serves 12.

Italian Sausage Vegetable Soup

2 pounds Italian sausage cut into 1-inch pieces
1½ cups chopped onion
3 tablespoons minced garlic
8 potatoes peeled and cut into pieces
4 cups cut up baby carrots
2 quarts vegetable juice
1½ teaspoons Italian seasoning
½ teaspoon basil
½ teaspoon sea salt
¼ teaspoon pepper

Brown the Italian sausage pieces in a 6-quart stock pot; add the onion and garlic and cook until onion is translucent. Add the potatoes, carrots and vegetable juice. Bring to a boil; reduce heat and simmer for 15-20 minutes. Stir in the Italian seasoning, basil, sea salt and pepper. Continue to simmer until the vegetables are tender. Serves 12.

Desserts

Apple Crisp, **page 115**

Toasted Coconut

½ cup shredded, unsweetened coconut

Preheat oven to 375°. Place coconut in a shallow baking dish. Bake approximately 10-12 minutes or until golden brown. Makes ½ cup.

Toasted Pecans

1 cup unsalted pecan pieces

Preheat oven to 350°. On a baking sheet, spread nut meats out evenly. Bake until lightly browned and toasted, approximately 5-6 minutes. Cool completely. Makes 1 cup.

Vanilla Pudding

¼ cup plus 1 tablespoon potato starch flour
⅔ cup soy creamer
2 beaten egg yolks
⅔ cup sucanat
¼ teaspoon sea salt
2 cups vanilla soy milk
2¼ teaspoons vanilla

Mix potato starch flour with soy creamer and egg yolks; whisk until smooth. Mix sucanat, sea salt and soy milk in a medium saucepan. Simmer over medium heat for 5-6 minutes, stirring often. Add 1 cup of milk mixture to egg yolk mixture and whisk gently. Pour egg yolk mixture into saucepan with remainder of cream mixture. Continue to cook on medium heat, stirring constantly. Remove from heat and stir in vanilla. Cool slightly; cover with wax paper to prevent a hard skin from forming. Chill and serve. Makes approximately 3½ cups.

Apple Crisp

4 medium tart apples, peeled and sliced (approximately 4 cups)
¾ cup sucanat
1 teaspoon molasses
½ cup gluten-free oat flour
½ cup Gluten Free Oats
⅓ cup clarified butter, softened
¾ teaspoon cinnamon
¾ teaspoon nutmeg

Preheat oven to 375°. Butter an 8-by-8-inch square pan. Spread apple slices in pan. In a small bowl combine remaining ingredients and sprinkle over apples. Bake for 30 minutes until golden brown and apples are tender. Serves 6-8.

Individual Toasted Coconut Puddings

½ cup turbinado sugar

3 tablespoons potato starch flour

3 cups vanilla soy milk

3 beaten egg yolks

1 tablespoon clarified butter

1 teaspoon vanilla

½ teaspoon coconut extract

¾ cup toasted coconut

⅔ cup dairy-free chocolate chips (optional)

In a saucepan over medium-low heat, combine turbinado sugar and potato starch flour, stir in vanilla soy milk and egg yolks. Stir mixture until smooth. Bring to a boil, stirring constantly until mixture begins to thicken, 2-3 minutes. Remove from heat, add clarified butter, vanilla and coconut extract. Spoon equal amounts into individual baking dishes and top with toasted coconut and dairy-free chocolate chips if desired. This may be served at any temperature desired. Serves 4

Streusel Topping

½ cup clarified butter, melted

½ cup sucanat

1 teaspoon cinnamon

1 tablespoon brown rice flour

⅓ cup chopped pecans (optional)

Blend all ingredients in a small bowl. Then sprinkle on top of muffins, cakes or cobblers before baking. Makes 1 to 1⅓ cups.

Poached Peaches in Wine Sauce

8 fresh peaches

¼ teaspoon allspice

½ teaspoon lemon peel

½ teaspoon cinnamon

2 cups sweet, fruity wine (I use a strawberry)

Peel, pit and cut the peaches into fourths or halves, whichever you prefer, and set aside. In a small bowl combine the allspice, lemon peel and cinnamon; set aside. Pour 2 cups of wine into a small saucepan and bring to a boil. Stir in the spices and the peaches and boil for 3 minutes. Remove the peaches from the liquid and set aside. Bring the liquid mixture back to a boil and simmer for 13-15 minutes longer or until the liquid is reduced by half. Pour the wine sauce over the peaches and serve warm or cold over ice cream. Serves 8.

*G*lazed Fresh Fruit

2 cups freshly sliced peaches

1 cup sliced strawberries

1 cup blueberries

1 cup green grapes, halved

⅓ cup orange juice

¼ cup 100% fruit orange marmalade

1 tablespoon honey

In a large bowl combine the peaches, strawberries, blueberries and grapes; set aside. In a small mixing bowl combine the orange juice and orange marmalade and stir until smooth. Add the honey and stir again until ingredients are well combined. Pour orange juice mixture over the fresh fruit and fold until all the fruit is completely coated. Chill and serve. Serves 8-10.

*B*lueberry Bread Pudding

½ cup clarified butter, softened

2 cups sucanat

8 eggs

2 cups fresh blueberries

3 tablespoons lemon juice

10 slices Millet & Flax Bread cubed (day old works best)

Preheat oven to 350°. In a large mixing bowl cream clarified butter and sucanat. Add eggs, one at a time, beating well after each one. Stir in blueberries and lemon juice. Fold in bread cubes. Pour into a buttered 9-by-13-inch baking dish. Bake uncovered for 35 minutes or until golden brown. Serves 12.

*F*resh Peach Sauce

½ bushel fresh peaches, stones removed, peeled and sliced

1 teaspoon vitamin C powder, divided

In a 4-quart casserole place ½ of the sliced peaches; cook on high in the microwave for 6-8 minutes or until the peaches are tender; stir halfway through the cooking time. Remove from oven and sprinkle with ½ teaspoon of the vitamin C powder. Place the peaches 1½-2 cups at a time in a blender and pulse on puree until the mixture is completely smooth. Place in pint freezer containers and refrigerate for immediate use or freeze for up to 6 months. Repeat the process with the remaining peaches and vitamin C powder. Makes approximately 8 quarts.

Peach Cobbler

- 2 cups sliced peaches
- 4 tablespoons clarified butter, softened
- 1¾ cup sucanat, divided
- 1 teaspoon baking powder
- ¾ teaspoon sea salt, divided
- 1 cup Basic Baking Mix
- ½ cup vanilla soy milk
- 1 tablespoon potato starch flour
- 1 cup water

Preheat oven to 350°. In a 9-by-9-inch baking pan place the peaches; set aside. In a small mixing bowl combine the clarified butter and ¾ cup of the sucanat until creamy. Stir in the baking powder, ½ teaspoon of the sea salt and baking mix. Gently stir in the vanilla soy milk and stir until smooth and blended. Pour batter evenly over the top of the peaches. In a small bowl combine the potato starch flour, the remaining sucanat and remaining sea salt. After blended, sprinkle the mixture evenly over the batter. Pour the water over the top of the entire peach and batter mixture and bake for 50-55 minutes or until golden and bubbly. Serves 8.

Strawberry Rhubarb Crisp

- 10 ounces frozen rhubarb
- 24 ounces sliced strawberries (may be frozen)
- 2¼ cup turbinado sugar, divided
- ¾ cup Basic Baking Mix
- ½ cup sweet rice flour
- 1 cup sorghum flour
- 1 cup clarified butter, melted

Preheat oven to 350°. In a 9–by-13-inch baking dish place the rhubarb and strawberries. Pour 2 cups of the turbinado sugar on top of the fruit; set aside. In a small mixing bowl combine the baking mix, sweet rice flour, sorghum flour and remaining ¼ cup turbinado sugar. Stir in the clarified butter and mix with a fork until blended. Spread the flour mixture over the top of the fruit and bake for 20-25 minutes or until golden and bubbly. Serves 8.

Butter Pecan Sundaes

- 4 scoops vanilla nondairy frozen dessert, soy, rice or coconut
- 8 tablespoons Butter Pecan Syrup, warmed (See Sauces & Such, page 106)
- 1 tablespoon chopped, toasted pecans

Place one scoop nondairy dessert in 4 separate dessert dishes. Top each scoop with 2 tablespoons of the Butter Pecan Syrup and ¼ tablespoon of the chopped pecans. Serve immediately. Serves 4.

Dark Chocolate Butter Pecan Sundaes

4 scoops chocolate nondairy frozen dessert, soy, rice or coconut

2 tablespoons dairy-free chocolate chips

8 tablespoons Butter Pecan Syrup, warmed (See Sauces & Such, page 106)

4 tablespoons Chocolate Sauce

1 tablespoon chopped, toasted pecans

Place one scoop nondairy dessert in 4 separate dessert dishes. Top each scoop with ½ tablespoon chocolate chips, 2 tablespoons Butter Pecan Syrup and 1 tablespoon Chocolate Sauce. Sprinkle top of each dessert with ¼ tablespoon chopped pecans. Serve immediately. Serves 4.

Blueberry Cobbler

Filling:

½ cup maple syrup

4 teaspoons tapioca flour

4 cups fresh blueberries

Pour maple syrup into a medium sauce pan over medium heat. Stir in tapioca flour and continue to stir until mixture is smooth. Add blueberries and bring mixture to a boil; reduce heat and simmer for 5-6 minutes or until liquid is glassy and thickened.

Topping:

½ cup Basic Baking Mix

¾ cup sorghum flour

2 teaspoons corn-free baking powder

¼ teaspoon sea salt

2 tablespoons sucanat

2 tablespoons canola oil

½ cup vanilla soymilk

½ teaspoon vanilla

In a small mixing bowl combine the baking mix, sorghum flour, baking powder, sea salt and sucanat. Stir in the canola oil, soymilk and vanilla until blended.

Preheat oven to 375°. Prepare the cobbler filling; set aside. Prepare cobbler topping; set aside. Pour the cobbler filling evenly into a 9-by-13-inch baking dish. Top the filling with the cobbler topping by dropping evenly over the top by tablespoons. Bake for 30-35 minutes or until golden brown. Serves 8.

Coconut Rhubarb Strawberry Cobbler

Filling:

> ¾ cup maple syrup
>
> 4 teaspoons tapioca flour
>
> 1½ cups chunked rhubarb
>
> 2½ cups sliced strawberries

Pour maple syrup into a medium sauce pan set at medium heat. Stir in tapioca flour and continue to stir until mixture is smooth. Add rhubarb and strawberries and bring mixture to a boil; reduce heat and simmer for 5-6 minutes or until liquid is glassy and thickened.

Topping:

> ½ cup sorghum flour
>
> ½ cup sucanat
>
> ¼ teaspoon corn-free baking powder
>
> ⅛ teaspoon sea salt
>
> ½ cup unsweetened coconut
>
> ¼ cup chopped pecans
>
> 4 tablespoons clarified butter

Preheat oven to 350°. Prepare rhubarb strawberry filling; set aside. In a small mixing bowl combine the sorghum flour, sucanat, baking powder and sea salt. Stir dry ingredients to combine well. Stir in coconut and pecans and combine. Pour the fruit mixture evenly into a 9-by-13-inch buttered baking dish. Sprinkle the coconut topping evenly over the fruit. Cut clarified butter into pieces and place evenly over top of cobbler. Bake for 30 minutes or until golden. Serves 8.

Brownies, Bars & Cookies

Chocolate Chip Bars, **page 123**

Lemon Bars

Crust:

8 tablespoons clarified butter, softened
¼ cup sucanat
1 cup Basic Baking Mix

Filling:

4 eggs
1½ cups sucanat
Juice of 2 large lemons
¼ cup Basic Baking Mix
½ teaspoon corn-free baking powder
1 tablespoon chopped lemon zest

Preheat oven to 375°. For crust, mix clarified butter and sucanat until creamy. Gradually add baking mix and mix well. Press mixture firmly into a 9-by-9-inch square pan and bake for 10-12 minutes; cool slightly. Meanwhile, in a medium mixing bowl, beat eggs, sucanat, lemon juice, baking mix and corn-free baking powder until the mixture is quite bubbly. Pour over the warm crust and bake for 15 minutes until set. Cool completely and sprinkle with lemon zest before serving. Cut into 9 pieces. Serves 9.

Butterscotch Brownies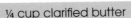

¼ cup clarified butter

1 cup sucanat

1 teaspoon molasses

1 teaspoon vanilla

2 tablespoons soy milk

1 egg

1 cup Basic Baking Mix

½ cup chopped pecans (optional)

1 teaspoon corn-free baking powder

½ teaspoon sea salt

Preheat oven to 350°. Butter the bottom and sides of an 8-by-8-inch square baking dish. Melt clarified butter in a small saucepan over low heat. Remove from heat and add sucanat, molasses, vanilla, soy milk and egg. Stir until well combined. Then add baking mix, pecans, corn-free baking powder and sea salt. Spread mixture into the baking dish evenly and bake 25 minutes or until golden brown. Cool baking dish on a wire rack for 5-10 minutes and cut the brownies while still slightly warm. Serves 8.

Cocoa Brownies

1 cup Basic Baking Mix

1 teaspoon xanthan gum

½ cup plus 2 tablespoons cocoa powder

4 eggs

1¾ cups sucanat

⅛ teaspoon sea salt

1 cup plus 2 tablespoons canola oil

1 teaspoon vanilla

Preheat oven to 350°. In a small bowl, mix together baking mix, xanthan gum and cocoa. Set aside. In another bowl beat eggs, sucanat and sea salt on medium speed until smooth and blended. Add canola oil and vanilla and mix again until blended. Carefully fold in dry ingredients until combined. Pour into a buttered 9-by-13-inch pan and bake for 20-25 minutes or until set. Makes 15 brownies.

Double Chocolate Chip Brownies

1 cup Basic Baking Mix

1 teaspoon xanthan gum

½ cup plus 2 tablespoons cocoa powder

4 eggs

1¾ cups sucanat

⅛ teaspoon sea salt

1 cup plus 2 tablespoons canola oil

1 teaspoon vanilla

1 cup dairy-free chocolate chips

Preheat oven to 350°. In a small bowl, mix together baking mix, xanthan gum and cocoa. Set aside. In another bowl beat eggs, sucanat and sea salt on medium speed until smooth and blended. Add canola oil and vanilla and mix again until blended. Carefully fold in dry ingredients until mixed. Stir in dairy-free chocolate chips. Pour into a buttered 9-by-13-inch pan and bake for 20-25 minutes or until set. Makes 15 brownies.

Chocolate Chip Bars

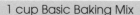
1 cup Basic Baking Mix
1 teaspoon xanthan gum
4 eggs
1¾ cups sucanat
⅛ teaspoon sea salt
1 cup canola oil
1 teaspoon vanilla
1¼ cups dairy-free chocolate chips

Preheat oven to 350°. In a small bowl, combine baking mix and xanthan gum. Set aside. In a large mixing bowl beat together eggs, sucanat and sea salt on medium speed until smooth and blended. Add canola oil and vanilla and blend on low for 1 minute. Fold in dry ingredients and blend. Stir in dairy-free chocolate chips. Pour into a buttered 9-by-13-inch pan and bake for 20-25 minutes or until golden brown. Makes 15 bars.

Cinna-Vanilla Blondies

1 cup plus 1 tablespoon Basic Baking Mix
1 teaspoon xanthan gum
½ teaspoon cinnamon
4 eggs
½ cup honey
½ cup turbinado sugar
⅛ teaspoon sea salt
1 cup canola oil
2 teaspoons vanilla

Preheat oven to 350°. In a small bowl combine baking mix, xanthan gum and cinnamon. Set aside. In a large mixing bowl beat together eggs, honey, turbinado sugar and sea salt on medium speed until smooth and blended. Add canola oil and vanilla and beat 1 minute to combine. Fold in dry ingredients until combined. Pour into a buttered 9–by-13-inch pan and bake for 20-25 minutes or until golden brown. Makes 15 blondies.

Baking Tip! Overmixing brownie batter can cause the brownie's texture to be less tender.

Low Sugar Oatmeal Cookies

1 cup agave nectar

½ cup canola margarine

½ cup unsweetened applesauce

1 teaspoon baking soda

1 teaspoon cinnamon

1 teaspoon vanilla

½ teaspoon corn-free baking powder

½ teaspoon sea salt

 2 eggs

3 cups Gluten Free Oats

1 cup gluten-free oat flour

1 cup raisins or dairy-free chocolate chips (optional)

Preheat oven to 375°. Mix agave nectar, margarine, applesauce, baking soda, cinnamon, vanilla, corn-free baking powder, salt and eggs until well combined. Stir in oats and oat flour, raisins or dairy-free chocolate chips if desired. Drop by rounded tablespoons about 2 inches apart on a buttered cookie sheet. Bake 9-11 minutes or until golden brown. Cool on wire rack. Makes approximately 3 dozen cookies.

Coconut Oatmeal Bars

 4 cups Gluten Free Oats

1 cup sucanat

1 teaspoon molasses

1 teaspoon sea salt

1 cup shredded coconut (unsweetened)

 ¾ cup clarified butter, melted

¾ cup orange marmalade 100% fruit spread

Preheat oven to 425°. In a large bowl combine the oats and sucanat. Add molasses, sea salt, coconut and melted clarified butter; stir to combine. Stir in orange marmalade and mix well. Pour mixture into a buttered jelly roll pan and bake for 15-17 minutes or until set. Makes 15 bars.

Sweet Potato Spice Bars

4 eggs

2 cups sucanat

1 cup canola oil

15 ounces sweet potato purée or sweet potato baby food

 1 cup Basic Baking Mix

½ cup sorghum flour

2 teaspoons corn-free baking powder

2 teaspoons ground cinnamon

1 teaspoon baking soda

½ teaspoon sea salt

½ teaspoon ground ginger

¼ teaspoon ground cloves

1 recipe Vanilla Cream Cheese Frosting, (See Pies, Cakes & Frostings, page 137)

¾ cup chopped pecans

Preheat oven to 350° and lightly oil the bottom and sides of a jelly roll pan with canola oil. In a mixing bowl beat eggs, sucanat, canola oil and sweet potatoes until smooth. Stir in baking mix, sorghum flour, corn-free baking powder, cinnamon, baking soda, sea salt, ginger and cloves. Spread batter evenly into pan. Bake 25-30 minutes or until browned lightly on top. Cool completely in pan on a wire rack (about 2 hours). Frost top with Vanilla Cream Cheese Frosting and sprinkle with chopped pecans. Cut into 7 rows by 7 rows for bars and store in the refrigerator. Makes 49 (1-by-1-inch) bars.

Pecan Pie Bars

½ cup clarified butter, melted

¾ cup Gluten Free Oats

2 tablespoons gluten-free oat flour

½ cup quinoa flakes

¼ cup pecan meal

1 cup sucanat, divided

3 eggs

½ cup agave nectar

½ cup honey

1½ tablespoons molasses

1 teaspoon vanilla

1½ cups pecan pieces

Preheat oven to 350°. In a medium mixing bowl combine clarified butter, oats, oat flour, quinoa flakes, pecan meal and ½ cup of the sucanat. Stir well to blend; then pat evenly into an unbuttered 9-by-13-inch baking dish. Set aside. In another mixing bowl combine the remaining ½ cup sucanat, eggs, agave nectar, honey, molasses and vanilla. Stir by hand until thoroughly combined. Spread filling evenly over crust and sprinkle with the pecan pieces. Bake for 30-35 minutes, until filling is set in the middle. Cool completely before serving. Serves 15-18.

Freezer Tip! Don't lose things in your freezer. Keep an inventory list on the front of your freezer so you know what you have on hand. Check things off when you use them and add to the list when replenishing.

Caramel Coconut Oatmeal Bars

1 cup Gluten Free Oats
1 cup coconut
½ cup sucanat
1 teaspoon molasses
¼ cup clarified butter, melted
1 cup agave nectar
1 teaspoon vanilla
½ teaspoon sea salt
6 ounces dairy-free chocolate chips

Preheat oven to 400°. In a large bowl combine oats, coconut and sucanat. Stir slightly to blend. Stir in molasses, melted clarified butter, agave nectar, vanilla and sea salt; mix well and then pat mixture evenly into an 8–by–8-inch buttered baking dish. Bake for 8-10 minutes. Remove from oven and sprinkle with dairy-free chocolate chips. Allow the chips to melt and then spread them evenly over the bars. Refrigerate for about 1 hour; cut into 2-by-1-inch squares to serve. Makes 32 bars.

Quinoa Honey Cookies

½ cup honey
⅓ cup sucanat
1 teaspoon molasses
½ cup sunflower nut butter
1 teaspoon vanilla
1 cup white rice flour
¾ cup quinoa flakes
1 teaspoon baking soda
¼ teaspoon sea salt

Preheat oven to 350°. In a large mixing bowl beat honey, sucanat, molasses, sunflower nut butter and vanilla until smooth and creamy; set aside. In a small bowl combine the white rice flour, quinoa flakes, baking soda and sea salt. Add the dry mixture to the creamed mixture 1 cup at a time, stirring well to combine ingredients. Drop by teaspoonfuls on a baking sheet about 2 inches apart. Bake 12-13 minutes or until lightly browned. Makes approximately 24 cookies.

Maple Chocolate Chip Cookies

5 cups Basic Baking Mix
1¼ teaspoon baking soda
½ teaspoon vitamin C powder
1¼ cup maple syrup
¼ cup maple sugar
1 cup canola oil
¼ cup vanilla soymilk
1½ cups dairy-free chocolate chips

126

Preheat oven to 375°. Combine baking mix, baking soda and vitamin C powder in a large bowl; set aside. Mix the maple syrup, maple sugar, canola oil and vanilla soymilk and stir gradually into the dry ingredients. Stir in the dairy- free chocolate chips. Drop by tablespoonfuls onto a buttered cookie sheet. Flatten the portions to about ¼ inch thickness with fingers. Bake 9-12 minutes or until slightly browned. Makes 3-4 dozen cookies.

$\mathcal{G}$olden Cashew Cherry Granola Bars

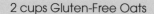
2 cups Gluten-Free Oats
1½ cups raw cashew nuts
½ cup honey
¼ cup sucanat
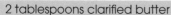
2 tablespoons clarified butter
½ teaspoon sea salt
2 teaspoons vanilla
1¼ cup mix of golden raisins and dried cherries
¾ cup raisins plumped in hot water for 5 minutes then drained

Preheat oven to 350°. Butter a 9-by-9-inch baking dish; set aside. On a jelly roll pan spread the oats and cashews evenly. Place in the oven for 15 minutes; stir occasionally to toast. In a medium saucepan combine the honey, sucanat, clarified butter, sea salt and vanilla. Cook on medium heat, stirring occasionally until the sucanat is completely dissolved. When the oat mixture is done, remove from oven and reduce heat to 300°. Immediately place the oat mixture into a mixing bowl, add the dried fruit and pour the liquid mixture over it. Stir until all ingredients are completely coated. Turn the mixture into the buttered baking dish and press it down evenly. Bake for 25 minutes, remove and cool completely. Cut into squares and store in an airtight container for up to 10 days. Makes 16-18 bars.

$\mathcal{O}$atmeal Chocolate Chip Bars

½ cup palm shortening
1½ cups sucanat
2 eggs
1½ teaspoons vanilla
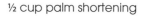
1 cup Basic Baking Mix
½ cup Gluten Free Oats
1 teaspoon corn-free baking powder
½ teaspoon sea salt
1 cup dairy-free chocolate chips

Preheat oven to 350°. With an electric mixer blend together palm shortening and sucanat until creamy. Add eggs and vanilla; continue mixing until smooth; set aside. In another bowl, combine the baking mix, oats, baking powder and sea salt. Fold dry ingredients into the egg mixture and stir until well combined. Stir in dairy-free chocolate chips. Spread evenly into a buttered 9-by-13-inch baking pan. Bake 25-30 minutes or until golden brown. Cool completely before cutting into bars. Makes 15-24 bars.

Pies, Cakes & **Frostings**

Sweet Potato Pie with Maple Pecan Glaze, **page 139**

Strawberry Pie

    1½ cups apple juice concentrate
    1 (20-ounce) package frozen strawberries, drained
    ¼ cup strawberry juice from ½ cup mashed berries
    ¼ cup plus 2 teaspoons quick-cooking tapioca
    1 baked Old-Fashioned (contains egg) or Oat Pie Crust (See Pies, Cakes & Frostings, pages 128 & 129)

Put apple juice in a small saucepan. Mash ½ cup strawberries through a sieve to make juice. Add strawberry juice to apple juice. Boil juices down to ¾ cup in volume. Add drained strawberries and quick-cooking tapioca; let stand for 5 minutes. Boil mixture for 5 minutes. Cool for 10 minutes and pour into a cooled, baked pie crust. Chill for at least 2 hours before serving. Serves 8.

Oat Pie Crust

    2 cups gluten-free oat flour
    1 cup Gluten Free Oats
    ½ teaspoon sea salt
    ½ cup canola oil
    ¼ cup maple syrup

Preheat oven to 400°. In a large bowl combine oat flour, oats and sea salt. Add canola oil and blend in thoroughly. Add maple syrup and mix dough until it starts to stick together. (Add 1-2 teaspoons of water if necessary). Divide dough into halves and pat nicely into 2 (9-inch) pie plates. Prick crust with a fork and bake for 15-20 minutes or until the bottom of the crust begins to brown. Makes 2 (9-inch) single pie crusts.

Old-Fashioned Pie Crust

1½ cups Basic Baking Mix
4 tablespoons sweet rice flour
2 teaspoons powdered sucanat
¼ teaspoon sea salt
9 tablespoons cold clarified butter
1 egg
1½ teaspoons apple cider vinegar
3 tablespoons ice water

Preheat oven to 400°. Combine baking mix, sweet rice flour, sucanat and sea salt. Slice clarified butter into pieces then using your fingers or a pastry blender, work clarified butter into dry mixture until it becomes coarse and crumbly. Make a well in the center of the mix and add the egg. Work the egg into mixture and add apple cider vinegar and ice water until a soft dough forms. Refrigerate for about 15 minutes if dough is too soft to roll out. For a prebaked crust, bake about 15 minutes. Makes 1 single 9-inch pie crust.

Grandma Iva's Pecan Pie

1 unbaked No Roll Pie Crust (recipe follows)
⅔ cup sucanat
⅓ teaspoon sea salt
⅓ cup clarified butter, melted
3 eggs, lightly beaten
1 tablespoon molasses
½ cup agave nectar
½ cup honey
1¼ cups pecan halves

Preheat oven to 375°. In a mixing bowl combine sucanat and sea salt. Pour in clarified butter and eggs; stir lightly. Add molasses, agave nectar and honey. Mix well. Stir in pecan halves and pour into pie shell. Bake for 40 minutes or until pie filling is set. Serves 8.

No Roll Pie Crust

1¼ cups Basic Baking Mix
¼ cup sweet rice flour
2 tablespoons turbinado sugar
2 tablespoons pecan meal
½ teaspoon sea salt
½ cup canola oil

Preheat oven to 375°. In a mixing bowl combine baking mix, sweet rice flour, sugar, pecan meal and sea salt. Pour canola oil into dry ingredients and mix well with a fork. Pat crust into a 9-inch pie plate. Fill the crust and bake for 20 minutes or bake the unfilled crust for 12 minutes. Makes 1 (9-inch) crust.

Boston Cream Pie

This is one of Wesley's favorites, and he has chosen it as his birthday cake many times!

Cake:

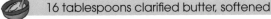

1⅓ cups brown rice flour

⅔ cup potato starch flour

2 tablespoons sweet rice flour

2 teaspoons Egg Replacer

1 teaspoon corn-free baking powder

½ teaspoon xanthan gum

¼ teaspoon sea salt

16 tablespoons clarified butter, softened

1 cup sucanat

¼ cup plus 2 tablespoons vanilla soy milk

4 eggs

1 recipe Vanilla Pudding (See Desserts, page 115)

1 recipe Chocolate Ganache (See Pies, Cakes & Frostings, page 133)

Preheat oven to 350 °. Line two 8-inch round pans with parchment and butter generously. In a mixing bowl combine brown rice flour, potato starch flour, sweet rice flour, Egg Replacer, corn-free baking powder, xanthan gum and sea salt. Set aside. With an electric mixer beat clarified butter until fluffy and lighter in color. Add sucanat and beat on medium speed until combined and fluffy, about 4 minutes. Add eggs, one at a time and beat until smooth. Slowly add dry ingredients to blend and then add vanilla soy milk. Pour batter evenly into two prepared cake pans. Bake for 15-20 minutes or until a toothpick comes out clean when pricked. Let cool in the pan for 10-15 minutes before turning onto a cake platter.

To assemble the Boston Cream Pie, place one layer of cake on serving platter; spread the pudding over that layer. Place the second layer of cake on top of first. Then, carefully spread the ganache over the top evenly and allow it to spill over the edges of the cake. Serve immediately. Serves 8-12.

Mayo-Cocoa Cake

1 cup Basic Baking Mix

¾ cup sucanat

¼ cup unsweetened cocoa

1 teaspoon corn-free baking powder

1 teaspoon baking soda

1 cup canola mayonnaise

1 cup water

Mix baking mix, sucanat, cocoa powder, corn-free baking powder and baking soda in a large mixing bowl. Add canola mayonnaise and mix well. Place batter in a buttered 9-by-13-inch backing dish and bake for 20-25 minutes. Serves 12.

$\mathcal{N}$o-Cheese Cheesecake

Crust:

¾ cup Gluten Free Oats
½ cup quinoa flakes
¼ cup almond meal
½ cup plus 2 tablespoons powdered sucanat
½ cup clarified butter, melted

Preheat oven to 375°. In a small mixing bowl combine oats, quinoa flakes, almond meal and powdered sucanat. Stir to mix well. Slowly stir in melted clarified butter until mixture is moistened. Pat by hand into a 9-by-13-inch baking dish. Set aside.

Filling:

16 ounces cream cheese substitute, rice or soy at room temperature
¾ cup powdered sucanat
¼ cup sucanat
2 beaten eggs
1 teaspoon vanilla

In a mixing bowl beat cream cheese substitute on medium speed until smooth. Add powdered sucanat, sucanat, eggs and vanilla and continue to blend until well combined. Pour mixture evenly over crust and bake for 15-20 minutes. Cool completely before serving. This "cheese" cake is great topped with Chocolate Ganache, See Pies, Cakes & Frostings, page 133, or served with assorted fresh fruit. Serves 12.

Creamy Butter Cake

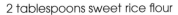 1⅓ cups brown rice flour

⅔ cup potato starch flour

2 tablespoons sweet rice flour

2 teaspoons Egg Replacer

1 teaspoon corn-free baking powder

½ teaspoon xanthan gum

¼ teaspoon sea salt

16 tablespoons clarified butter, softened

1 cup sucanat

4 eggs

¼ cup plus 2 tablespoons vanilla soy milk

Preheat oven to 350°. Line two 8-inch round pans with parchment paper and butter generously. In a mixing bowl combine brown rice flour, potato starch flour, sweet rice flour, Egg Replacer, corn-free baking powder, xanthan gum and sea salt. Set aside. With an electric mixer beat clarified butter until fluffy and lighter in color. Add sucanat and beat on medium speed until combined and fluffy, about 4 minutes. Add eggs, one at a time, and beat until smooth. Slowly add dry ingredients to blend and then add vanilla soy milk. Pour batter evenly into two prepared cake pans. Bake for 15-20 minutes or until a toothpick comes out clean when pricked. Let cool in the pan for 10-15 minutes before turning onto a cake platter. Serves 8.

Chocolate Frosting

1½ cups powdered sucanat

5 tablespoons cocoa powder

2-3 tablespoons vanilla rice milk

Combine powdered sucanat and cocoa in a small bowl. Slowly stir in rice milk, adding a bit more if needed for consistency. Stir until smooth then spread onto the cake, muffin or cupcake of your choice. Each recipe of frosting will cover a 9-by-9-inch double layer cake or a 9-by-13-inch sheet cake.

Chocolate Buttercream Frosting

⅓ cup plus 2 tablespoons clarified butter, softened

6 tablespoons cocoa

2 cups powdered sucanat

1 teaspoon vanilla

3 tablespoons vanilla soy milk

In a mixing bowl combine clarified butter and cocoa. With an electric mixer, beat in powdered sucanat, vanilla and vanilla soy milk. Beat on low for 1-2 minutes until frosting is smooth. One recipe will frost 2 (8- or 9-inch) cake layers or 1 (9–by–13-inch) cake.

Chocolate Applesauce Cake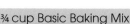

¾ cup Basic Baking Mix

⅓ cup arrowroot

1 teaspoon corn-free baking powder

1 teaspoon baking soda

¼ teaspoon xanthan gum

⅓ cup cocoa powder

2 egg whites

⅔ cup sucanat

⅓ cup vanilla soy milk

⅓ cup agave nectar

¼ cup unsweetened applesauce

Preheat oven to 350°. Line an 11–by–7-inch baking pan with parchment paper and butter lightly. In a small bowl mix together baking mix, arrowroot, corn-free baking powder, baking soda and xanthan gum. Then add cocoa powder a little bit at a time, stirring lightly to incorporate it into dry mixture. In a large mixing bowl beat the egg whites on medium-high until foamy. Slowly add sucanat and blend. Pour in vanilla soy milk, agave nectar and applesauce. Slowly blend dry ingredients into liquid ingredients. Pour batter into the baking pan and bake for 20-25 minutes or until a toothpick inserted comes out clean. Serves 8.

Mock Cream Cheese Frosting

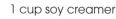

1 (3-ounce) package cream cheese substitute, rice or soy at room temperature

⅓ cup clarified butter, softened

1 teaspoon vanilla

2 cups powdered sucanat or powdered turbinado sugar

Beat cream cheese substitute and clarified butter in a mixing bowl with an electric mixer on low until smooth. Gradually beat in powdered sucanat or turbinado sugar 1 cup at a time on low until mixture is smooth. Each recipe of frosting will cover a 9-by-9-inch double layer cake or a 9-by-13-inch sheet cake.

Chocolate Ganache

1 cup soy creamer

1 cup dairy-free chocolate chips

In a small saucepan bring soy creamer to a boil while stirring constantly. Add dairy-free chocolate chips and stir until smooth and melted. Place mixture in freezer for 15-20 minutes, stirring twice in between. Remove from freezer when it has thickened slightly and will spread easily. Each recipe is adequate for a 9-by-9-inch double layer cake or a 9-by-13-inch sheet cake.

Coconut Cream Cake

- 1 teaspoon baking soda
- ½ teaspoon sea salt
- ½ cup sweet rice flour
- 1½ cups Basic Baking Mix
- 1 cup soy milk
- ½ teaspoon white vinegar
- 1½ cups clarified butter, softened
- 2 cups organic sugar or ground sucanat
- 5 eggs, separated
- 1 teaspoon vanilla
- 1 cup plus 2 tablespoons chopped pecans, divided
- 2¼ cups coconut, divided
- Coconut Cream Frosting (recipe follows)

Preheat oven to 350°. In a small mixing bowl combine the baking soda, sea salt, sweet rice flour and baking mix; set aside. In a liquid measuring cup combine the soy milk and the vinegar. Allow to set for about 3 minutes. Cream together the clarified butter and organic sugar or ground sucanat. Add egg yolks one at a time, stirring after each addition to combine the mixture. Slowly stir in the dry ingredients 1 cup at a time, alternating with the soy milk mixture and vanilla. Fold in 1 cup of the pecans and 2 cups of the coconut; set aside. Beat egg whites until fluffed and foamy. Fold the beaten egg whites into the cake batter gently. Pour batter evenly into 3 (9-inch) round cake pans and bake for 30 minutes. Remove partially cooled cakes from pans and allow to completely cool on a cooling rack. When cakes are cooled place the first cake on a serving platter and frost the top, place a second cake on top of that and frost its top, repeat with the third cake, then proceed to cover the sides of the cake with the frosting. When the process is completed, sprinkle the cake top with the remaining chopped pecans and the sides with the remaining coconut. Serves 12.

Coconut Cream Frosting

- 8 tablespoons clarified butter, softened
- 1 cup cream cheese substitute, rice or soy at room temperature.
- ¼ teaspoon coconut extract
- 1 teaspoon vanilla
- 3¼ cups powdered sucanat
- 2 tablespoons coconut

In a mixing bowl cream together the clarified butter and cream cheese substitute. Stir in the vanilla, coconut extract, powdered sucanat and coconut. Continue stirring until well blended. Makes enough frosting to cover a 9-by-9-inch double layer, a 9-by-13-inch sheet cake or 18-24 cupcakes.

Chocolate Chip Cookie Pie

2 cups Chocolate Chip Bar (See Brownies, Bars & Cookies, page 123) crumbs with two tablespoons reserved
⅓ cup clarified butter, melted
1 recipe Vanilla Pudding, (See Desserts, page 115)
Chocolate Sauce

In a 10-inch glass pie plate sprinkle the Chocolate Chip Bar crumbs. Pour in the melted clarified butter and press into a crust with a fork over the bottom of the pie plate only. Cook one recipe of Vanilla Pudding and cool for 20-25 minutes. Stir pudding and then pour it over the crumb crust. Sprinkle the top with the reserved crumbs and drizzle with Chocolate Sauce. Serves 6-8.

Cream Cheese Pie Crust

8 ounces softened cream cheese substitute, rice or soy
½ cup palm oil shortening or coconut oil
1 cup sorghum flour
1 cup white rice flour
½ teaspoon sea salt
¼ cup cold water

Preheat oven to 350°. Blend the cream cheese substitute and shortening together. Stir in the flours and sea salt until it becomes smooth. Divide into two equal portions. On a floured surface press out one portion and then press it into an 8-inch pie plate. Do the same for the other portion. Bake for 15-20 minutes or until golden brown. Or add the filling of choice and bake the amount of time called for in the recipe. Makes 2 (8-inch) pie crusts.

Cleaning Tip! An easy method for broiler pan clean up is to line the bottom broiler pan with aluminum foil. The foil can be gathered up and tossed away, leaving the pan easy to clean.

$\mathcal{B}$lueberry Tart

1 cup Basic Baking Mix
7 tablespoons clarified butter, softened

⅓ cup plus 2 tablespoons ground sucanat
3 cups fresh blueberries
¼ teaspoon ground cinnamon
1 tablespoon raspberry or strawberry 100% fruit spread

Preheat oven to 375°. Combine the baking mix, clarified butter and 2 tablespoons ground sucanat with your hands until the mixture holds together. Press mixture into the center of a 9-inch tart pan. Refrigerate for 5 minutes. Then evenly cover the bottom and sides of tart pan with the crust mixture. Combine the remaining ⅓ cup ground sucanat with 3 cups of the blueberries and cinnamon. Brush fruit spread over the tart crust; pour blueberry mixture into the pan. Bake 50 minutes or until the berries are soft. Remove from oven; remove the rim of the pan when cool. Serves 6-8.

$\mathcal{I}$ce Dream Brownie Pie

1 ⅔ cup Cocoa Brownie Crumbs (See Brownies, Bars & Cookies, page 122)
⅓ cup clarified butter, melted
1 pint chocolate or vanilla nondairy frozen dessert; soy, rice or coconut, softened
2 tablespoons dairy-free chocolate chips

Preheat oven to 350°. In a small bowl combine the brownie crumbs with the clarified butter with a fork. Place the crumb mixture in a 9-inch pie plate and press in evenly with a fork. Bake for 2-4 minutes then cool completely. When the crust is completely cooled, spread the softened soy dessert evenly into the crust. Place in the freezer for 45-60 minutes, top with dairy-free chocolate chips or Chocolate Sauce. Serves 6-8.

Baking Tip! No applesauce or bananas, and you want to make muffins? Use canned peaches or pears. Drain the fruit, then puree in the blender until smooth. Use the same amount of fruit puree as you would applesauce or mashed bananas. Wallah!

Chocolate Brownie Pie

2½ cups Cocoa Brownie Crumbs (See Brownies, Bars & Cookies, page 122)
5 tablespoons clarified butter, 3 melted, 2 softened
½ cup sucanat
2 tablespoons arrowroot
⅓ cup cocoa
2 cups soy milk
2 egg yolks, beaten well
1 teaspoon vanilla

Preheat oven to 350°. Place brownie crumbs and melted, clarified butter in a small mixing bowl and combine well with a fork. Pour the crumbs into a 9-inch pie plate and press them firmly and evenly on the bottom and sides of the pan. Bake for 5-6 minutes; remove from oven and set aside to cool completely. In a 2-quart sauce pan, combine the sucanat, arrowroot and cocoa. Gently mix with a fork to blend. Turn burner to medium-low heat and carefully stir the soy milk into the dry mixture. Continue stirring while mixture is heating and cook for 2-3 minutes. Stir in egg yolks and continue to cook while stirring constantly until mixture begins to boil. As it begins to bubble it will start to thicken. When thickening begins, remove from heat and stir in the vanilla and clarified butter. Cover with a piece of waxed paper and allow pudding to cool. Pour the pudding into the brownie crust after it is cooled and refrigerate for at least 1 hour before serving. Serves 6-8.

Vanilla Cream Cheese Frosting

4 ounces cream cheese substitute, rice or soy at room temperature
⅓ cup palm shortening
1¼ cup powdered sucanat
2 teaspoons vanilla

In a small bowl cream together the cream cheese substitute and the palm shortening. Slowly stir in the powdered sucanat and combine well. Stir in the vanilla and continue stirring until the mixture is smooth. Remember, when making your own powdered sucanat it will be a bit granular and not completely smooth like commercial powdered sugar. Makes frosting to cover 12-18 cupcakes or a 9-by-13-inch sheet cake.

Applesauce Spice Cupcakes

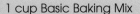

1 cup Basic Baking Mix
½ cup sorghum flour
¼ teaspoon baking powder
1 teaspoon baking soda
2 teaspoons cinnamon
1 teaspoon freshly grated nutmeg
¼ teaspoon ground cloves
½ teaspoon ginger
¼ teaspoon sea salt
1 tablespoon Egg Replacer
4 tablespoons warm water
1⅓ cup sucanat
⅓ cup plus 2 tablespoons palm shortening
1 tablespoon molasses
⅓ cup rice milk
½ teaspoon vanilla
¾ cup unsweetened applesauce

Preheat oven to 350°. Line muffin pans with foil-lined muffin cups; set aside. In a small mixing bowl combine the baking mix, sorghum flour, baking powder, baking soda, cinnamon, nutmeg, cloves, ginger and sea salt; set aside. In a small sauce dish or liquid measuring cup, place the Egg Replacer and whisk in the warm water until the mixture is smooth; set aside. In a large mixing bowl cream together the sucanat, palm shortening and molasses. Stir in the rice milk, vanilla and applesauce; continue stirring until well incorporated. Slowly stir in the Egg Replacer mixture and combine. Stir in the dry ingredients 1 cup at a time and continue stirring until completely combined. Pour batter into prepared muffin tins to make approximately ⅔ full. Bake for 18-20 minutes, until a toothpick comes out clean. Cool completely; frost with Vanilla Cream Cheese Frosting (See Pies, Cakes & Frostings page 137). Makes 12-18 cupcakes.

Vanilla Bean Tart

   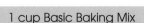

1 cup Basic Baking Mix
7 tablespoons clarified butter, softened
2 tablespoons turbinado sugar
½ a vanilla bean
½ teaspoon freshly grated nutmeg
¼ cup plus 1 tablespoon potato starch flour
2 ⅔ cup vanilla soy milk, divided
2 beaten egg yolks
⅔ cup turbinado sugar
¼ teaspoon sea salt
Freshly grated nutmeg
1½ teaspoons vanilla

Preheat oven to 375°. In a small bowl combine the baking mix, softened, clarified butter and turbinado sugar. With a fork or a pastry blender, cut the butter into the baking mix until crumbly. Then work the dough with your hands until it all holds together. Form dough into a ball and then place it in a tart pan. Press the dough down a little to begin forming a small circle. Place the pan with the dough in the refrigerator for 3-5 minutes to firm dough. Remove the pan and press the dough out evenly in the pan and up the sides. Place the crust in the oven and bake for 25 minutes or until the top begins to brown. While the crust is baking, slice the ½ of the vanilla bean through the top lengthwise. Do not penetrate through the whole bean, just through the top side. Flatten out the sides and then with a knife, scrape the insides of the bean into a small bowl. Add the nutmeg and set aside. In a large liquid measure place the potato starch flour, whisk in ⅔ cup of the soy milk and the beaten egg yolks until thoroughly mixed and smooth; set aside. In a medium sauce pan, combine the turbinado sugar, sea salt and remaining 2 cups soy milk. Simmer over medium heat, stirring often until the sugar is completely dissolved; about 4 minutes. Add 1 cup of the sweetened milk mixture to the egg mixture and whisk together gently. Slowly combine the entire egg mixture with the remaining sweetened milk. Whisk gently to ensure smoothness and cook on medium heat stirring constantly until the mixture begins to thicken. Reduce heat to low and add the vanilla bean and nutmeg mixture. Remove from heat and add the vanilla stirring well to combine. Cool slightly and pour into the baked tart crust, sprinkle with nutmeg if desired. Serve warm or cold. Serves 8.

$\int$orghum Flour Pie Crust

1 cup sorghum flour
½ cup Basic Baking Mix
2 teaspoons sucanat
1 teaspoon sea salt
½ cup clarified butter, completely softened
2 tablespoons vanilla soy milk

Preheat oven to 400°. Place flour, baking mix, sucanat and sea salt in a 9-inch pie plate. Stir to combine dry ingredients. Add the softened, clarified butter and stir with a fork to blend. Stir in the soy milk and continue to stir until completely combined. Pat the mixture into the bottom and up the sides of the pie plate. Prick the bottom of the crust two or three times with the fork and bake for 12-15 minutes or until golden brown. Use as directed in favorite pie recipe. Makes 1 (9-inch) pie crust.

$\int$weet Potato Pie with Maple Pecan Glaze

2 cups peeled, cooked and mashed sweet potatoes
1¼ cup sucanat, divided
6 tablespoons clarified butter, 4 tablespoons melted, 2 tablespoons softened
2 beaten eggs
1 teaspoon vanilla
¼ teaspoon sea salt
¼ teaspoon cinnamon
¼ teaspoon ginger
1 cup plus 2 tablespoons soy creamer, divided
¼ cup maple syrup
1 cup pecan pieces
1 9-inch unbaked pie crust I use the Sorghum Flour Pie Crust. (See Pies, Cakes & Frostings, page 139)

Preheat oven to 350°. With an electric mixer, combine the sweet potatoes, 1 cup of the sucanat, melted clarified butter, eggs, vanilla, sea salt, cinnamon and ginger. Mix thoroughly. Add 1 cup of the soy creamer and continue mixing. Pour the sweet potato filling into the pie crust and bake for 35-45 minutes or until a toothpick inserted in the center comes out clean. Place the pie on a cooling rack after baking before topping with glaze. In a small saucepan over medium heat, place the softened clarified butter and melt. Add the remaining ¼ cup sucanat and cook until smooth, about 3 minutes, stirring constantly. Add the maple syrup and then stir in the remaining 2 tablespoons soy creamer. Remove from heat and stir in pecans. Allow mixture to cool for 1 minute and then spread over cooled pie. Allow topping to set completely before serving. Refrigerate leftovers. Serves 8.

*E*ggless Chocolate Cake

1⅓ cups sweet rice flour
⅔ cup potato starch flour
1⅓ cups tapioca starch
⅔ cup white rice flour
2 cups sucanat
¾ cup cocoa
1 teaspoon sea salt
2 teaspoons baking soda
2 teaspoons vanilla
2 cups cold water
2 teaspoons white vinegar

⅔ cup canola oil
1 tablespoon Chocolate Sauce

Preheat oven to 350°. In a mixing bowl combine the sweet rice flour, potato and tapioca starches, white rice flour, sucanat, cocoa, sea salt and baking soda. Stir lightly to combine ingredients. Gently stir in the vanilla, water, vinegar, canola oil and chocolate sauce. Stir gently to smooth batter. Pour batter into a buttered 9-by-13-inch baking pan and bake for 35-40 minutes or until a toothpick comes out clean after inserted into the middle of cake. Serves 12.

*S*weet Potato Whoopie Pies

12 tablespoons clarified butter (divided 8 tablespoons melted, 4 tablespoons softened)
1 cup sucanat
1 teaspoon molasses
2 eggs, lightly beaten
1 cup sweet potato puree
1 teaspoon ground cloves
1 teaspoon cinnamon
1 teaspoon ginger
1½ teaspoons vanilla, divided
1 teaspoon baking powder
1 teaspoon baking soda
¾ teaspoon sea salt

1 cup Basic Baking Mix
⅔ cup sorghum flour
4 ounces cream cheese substitute, rice or soy at room temperature
1 cup powdered sucanat

Preheat the oven to 350°. Line two baking sheets with parchment paper. In a large bowl whisk together the melted butter, sucanat and molasses until smooth. Whisk in the eggs, sweet potato puree, cloves, cinnamon, ginger, 1 teaspoon vanilla, baking powder, baking soda and sea salt. Carefully fold in the baking mix and sorghum flour. Using an ice cream scoop or tablespoon, drop 12 generous mounds of batter, spaced evenly, onto each baking sheet. Bake 10 minutes or until tops spring back when touched. Transfer to a cooling rack; cool completely. Meanwhile, cream together the softened butter and the cream cheese substitute on medium speed with an electric mixer. Add the powdered sucanat and the remaining ½ teaspoon vanilla; mix on low speed until blended, then beat on medium-high speed until fluffy, approximately 2 minutes. Spread the flat side of each of the 12 cakes with the frosting. Place 2 cakes together, icing to icing to create a sandwich. Serves 6.

Kidding Around in the **Kitchen**

Strawberry Scones, **page 147**

Kids in the kitchen can have lots of fun, and children with food allergies can receive an important education while learning their way around the kitchen. My son, Wesley, has logged lots of kitchen hours with me, and as a result he's learned how to take charge of his diet, he's learned the art of reading food labels, and he's learned how to protect himself from food allergens.

By popular demand, I include instruction on allergy-free eating and cooking for children in classes as I travel and teach, and I've developed fun finger foods and snacks tasty enough and easy enough for kids to prepare.

Come on—bring your kids into your kitchen no matter what kind of diet you follow. Trust me, kids can cook— even the allergy-free way!

Triple Chocolate Milk Shake

6 scoops chocolate nondairy frozen dessert, divided

1 cup chocolate soy milk, divided

 4 teaspoons Chocolate Sauce

Place 3 scoops of chocolate nondairy frozen dessert in a blender and pulse until smooth. Add ½ of chocolate soy milk and blend until smooth. Add remaining frozen dessert, milk and chocolate sauce. Blend until smooth; serve immediately. Serves 2.

Micro Chocolate Pudding

¼ cup cocoa

⅓ cup sucanat

⅛ teaspoon sea salt

3 tablespoons potato starch flour

2 cups vanilla soy milk

In a microwave safe bowl combine cocoa, sucanat, sea salt and potato starch flour. Add soy milk, ¼ cup at a time, stirring to mix smoothly after each addition. Heat the mixture in the microwave on high for 2-3 minutes; stir well. Cook an additional 4-6 minutes, stirring well after each minute of cooking. Remove from microwave when pudding is thickened. Cool pudding completely before serving. Serves 4.

Super Veggie Dip

¼ cup plain soy yogurt

3 teaspoons honey

 ¼ cup Tofu Sour Cream

1½ teaspoons mustard

In a small bowl stir all ingredients to combine. Chill and serve with a variety of raw vegetables or Crunchy Veggie Trees. See Kidding Around the Kitchen, page 142.

Crunchy Veggie Trees

3 cups broccoli florets

2 medium-sized carrots, peeled and sliced lengthwise

6 grape tomatoes cut in half

Place ½ a carrot on 4 individual plates. Arrange 3-4 broccoli florets on top of the carrot "tree trunk." Put 3 grape tomato halves around the broccoli florets for "berries." Serve with Super Veggie Dip, See Kidding Around in the Kitchen, page 142. Serves 4.

Pizza Snacks

8 slices Sami's Millet & Flax Bread
1 cup Pizza Sauce (See Sauces & Such, page 101)
1 teaspoon Italian seasoning
½ teaspoon parsley flakes
½ teaspoon sea salt
¼ teaspoon oregano
¾ teaspoon garlic powder
½ cup vegan Parmesan

Preheat oven to 350°. Place bread slices on a jelly roll pan lined with parchment paper. In a small bowl blend pizza sauce and spices; stir until combined. Spread sauce by teaspoonfuls; cover bread with desired amount. Top each slice with even amounts of the vegan Parmesan; bake 10-15 minutes or until bubbly and slightly browned. Serves 8.

Wesley's Egg Salad

10 hard-boiled eggs, shelled and sliced
1½ cups chopped celery
⅜ cup chopped onion
¾ cup canola mayonnaise
½ tablespoon plus 1 teaspoon balsamic vinegar
1¾ teaspoons crushed thyme
⅛ teaspoon pepper

Place sliced eggs in a large bowl and mash with a fork. Add celery and onion and set aside. In a small bowl, mix mayonnaise, balsamic vinegar, thyme and pepper. Add mayonnaise mixture to the egg mixture and stir to blend thoroughly. Serve with crackers or as a sandwich on bread. Serves 8.

Grandma's Great Garlic Mix

My mother—and Wesley's grandma—always made lots of snacks during the holidays and throughout the year. After Wesley's diagnosis, she also wanted him to have the same types of foods that we all shared. She came up with this recipe and sent it to Wesley because he had been feeling under the weather. He was excited that Grandma made a snack just for him, and it made him feel better too!

8 ounces sorghum cereal rings
6 cups rice cereal squares
1 package favorite rice or seed crackers broken into pieces
20 ounces pistachios, roasted, unsalted
8 ounces cashews, roasted, salted
8 ounces canola margarine, melted
4 tablespoons wheat-free tamari
2-3 tablespoons garlic powder
½ teaspoon paprika

Preheat oven to 225°. In a large bowl, combine the cereals, cracker pieces and nuts. Set aside. In a small bowl combine melted margarine with wheat-free tamari and spices. Stir to blend well. Pour over cereal and nut mix and stir to coat. Bake in a deep baking dish for 2 hours stirring every 15 minutes. Remove from oven and allow mixture to dry for 1 hour. Makes approximately 20 cups.

Favorite Fruit Dip

1 cup plain soy yogurt
⅛ cup maple syrup
⅛ teaspoon cinnamon

Combine all ingredients and serve with assorted fresh fruits. Makes approximately 1 cup.

Honey Lemonade

1½ cups honey
1½ cups fresh lemon juice at room temperature
3½ quarts water at room temperature

In a medium bowl blend honey and lemon juice until completely combined. Pour mixture into a 1-gallon pitcher. Add water to make 1 gallon. Chill and serve over ice with fresh lemon slices, if desired. Makes approximately 4 quarts.

Fruit Juice Finger Gelatin

4 tablespoons unflavored gelatin
4 cups 100% fruit juice, any flavor, divided (1 cup chilled)

In a medium bowl sprinkle gelatin over the 1 cup chilled juice. Let stand for 1-2 minutes. Boil remaining juice and stir in remaining gelatin until completely dissolved. Combine juices and pour into a 9-by-13-inch pan and chill until firm. Cut into 1- or 2-inch squares or cut with small cookie cutters and serve. Makes approximately 24 squares.

Fruit Juice Spritzers

This is not only a great alternative to sodas, but also a great summer refresher!

1 cup favorite 100% juice, chilled
¼ cup sparkling water, chilled

Pour juice and sparkling water into a drinking glass and lightly stir to blend. Serves 1.

Wesley's Cinna-Vanilla Tea

1 quart water
4 vanilla tea bags
¼ teaspoon cinnamon extract
4 teaspoons agave nectar

Pour the water into a 2-quart sauce pan and bring to a rolling boil. Place tea bags in water and remove from heat. Steep for 6 minutes; discard tea bags and stir in cinnamon extract and agave nectar. Chill and serve over ice. Serves 4.

Banana Protein Shake

    1 banana, peeled and halved
    1 scoop rice protein
    1½ scoops vanilla nondairy frozen dessert
    ½ cup vanilla soy milk
    Banana slices for garnish

Place banana, rice protein, nondairy dessert and vanilla soy milk in a blender. Pulse on puree several times until mixture is smooth. Pour into a tall glass and garnish with banana slices. Makes approximately 1 16-ounce serving.

Sunflower Fruit Dip

    ½ cup cream cheese substitute, rice or soy at room temperature
    3 tablespoons sunflower nut butter
    1 teaspoon agave nectar
    2 teaspoons sunflower seeds

In a small bowl combine the cream cheese substitute, rice or soy and sunflower nut butter. Combine well. Stir in the agave nectar; place in small serving bowl. Garnish with sunflower seeds. Makes approximately 1 cup.

Fresh Fruit Kabobs

    3-4 varieties of fresh fruits in season such as berries, oranges, different apple
    and grape varieties, mangoes – any kind of fruit you love!

Peel and wash fruits and cut into even chunks. Place alternating colored fruits on skewers, leaving approximately 1 inch of space at each end of the skewer. Serve chilled with fruit dip.

Candied Pecans

    1 egg white
    1 tablespoon water
    1 cup turbinado sugar
    ¾ teaspoon sea salt
    ½ teaspoon cinnamon
    3½ cups large pecan pieces or halves

Preheat oven to 250°. Butter a baking sheet; set aside. With an electric mixer blend the egg white and water until frothy; set aside. In a small bowl combine the turbinado sugar, sea salt and cinnamon. Stir the pecans into the egg white mixture until the nuts are coated evenly. Toss the nuts into the sugar mixture until well coated. Spread nuts evenly on buttered baking sheet. Bake for 1 hour, stirring every 15 minutes. Makes 3 ½ cups.

Tip! Cranberries are a good source of vitamin C and they contain other vitamins and minerals.

Strawberry Scones

5 tablespoons organic sugar, divided
1 cup chopped strawberries
1½ cups Basic Baking Mix
½ cup sorghum flour
2 teaspoons baking powder
¼ teaspoon sea salt
6 tablespoons clarified butter, slightly softened
⅔ cup soy creamer

Preheat oven to 400°. Stir 1 tablespoon of the sugar into the chopped strawberries and set aside. Combine 3 tablespoons of the sugar, baking mix, sorghum flour, baking powder and sea salt; stir to combine. Using a pastry blender, cut the butter into the dry mixture until it is slightly crumbly. Stir in the soy creamer until mixed well, then gently fold in the strawberries. Turn the dough onto a lightly floured surface and knead slightly until it is a bit firm, then form into a ¾-inch thick circle. Place on a small, buttered pizza pan and cut the circle of dough evenly into 6-8 wedges. Bake for 15 minutes; remove and sprinkle with remaining sugar. Continue baking for another 7-10 minutes. Serves 6-8.

Mock Peanut Butter Cup Treats

¼ cup soy nut butter
3 tablespoons agave nectar
2 tablespoons cream cheese substitute, rice or soy
1 teaspoon canola margarine
4 tablespoons dairy-free chocolate chips
4 slices Sami's Millet & Flax Bread

Preheat oven to 350°. In a small bowl combine the soy nut butter and agave nectar. Stir in the cream cheese substitute, rice or soy and canola margarine and mix until smooth. Add the chocolate chips and stir to distribute evenly. Spread the soy nut butter mixture evenly onto each of the 4 slices of bread. Bake for 4-5 minutes, or until the chocolate chips start to melt. Cut each piece of bread into four strips and serve. Serves 4.

Grandma's Snow Drop Snack Mix

This is yet another recipe created by Wesley's grandma. The original recipe was used at special occasions. Since it was not acceptable for us to have this and Wesley to be excluded, his grandma came up with this snack. It is always a special treat for Wesley and has been modified more than once to meet his specific dietary restrictions as they changed.

13½ cups square rice cereal
1½ cups dairy-free chocolate chips
¾ cup soy nut butter
6 tablespoons canola margarine
1½ teaspoons vanilla
3 cups powdered turbinado sugar

Place cereal in large bowl; set aside. Place chocolate chips, soy nut butter and canola margarine in a medium sauce pan. Stir over low heat until mixture is melted and smooth. Stir in vanilla. Pour over cereal and stir until well coated. Place powdered turbinado sugar and the cereal in a 2-gallon resealable bag. Shake the mixture well until all pieces are coated. Spread cereal mix onto waxed paper to cool. Refrigerate in an airtight container for maximum freshness. Makes approximately 15 cups.

Recipes By Category

Product **Resources**

Specialty, flavor-infused olive oils and balsamic vinegars

The Olive Branch
225 Toscana; Granger, IN 46530
Phone: (574) 855-1059
theolivebranch129@sbcglobal.net
www.theolivebranchinc.com

The Olive Branch products may also be found at:
Mattern's Butcher Shop and Corner Deli
201 South Main Street; Goshen, IN 46526
Phone: (574) 971-8906

Gluten- and corn-free millet & flax bread, hamburger and hot dog buns and lavash

Sami's Bakery
4914 East Busch Blvd.; Tampa, FL 33617
Phone: (813) 989-2722
www.samisbakery.com

Ricemellow Crème

Suzanne's Specialties
Phone: (800) 762-2135 Fax: (732) 828-8563
info@suzannes-specialties.com

Egg Replacer, soy milk powder, multiple gluten-free flour alternatives

Ener-G Foods
Phone: (800) 331-5222
www.ener-g.com

Beef and naturally smoked ham

Eagle Creek Farms Market
Carolyn Stoll
P.O. Box 1768; Warsaw, IN 46580
Phone: (800) 328-STEAK (7832); (574) 269-4708
info@eaglecreekfarms.com

Buffalo roasts, steaks and ground buffalo

Cook's Bison Ranch
5645 E 600S; Wolcottville, IN 46795
Phone: (866) 382-2356
www.cooksbisonranch.com

Available in the American Countryside Farmer's Market: Buffalo from Cook's Bison Ranch, several varieties of fresh meats, fresh produce, gluten-free products, unrefined sugars and sweeteners.

American Countryside Farmer's Market
27751 CR 26; Elkhart, IN 46517
Open 9 a.m. to 5 p.m. Thurs., Fri. & Sat. year round
Open 9 a.m. to 5 p.m. Wed. May-Labor Day
Phone: (877) 782-7386
www.americancountryside.us

Certified gluten-free oats

Gluten Free Oats
578 Lane 9; Powell, WY 82435
Phone: (307) 754-2058 Fax: (516) 723-0924
www.glutenfreeoats.com

Delicious, organically grown produce
Ridge Lane Farm

Roger and Lois Hooley
Phone: (574) 831-5824
www.ridgelanefarmproduce.com

Angus beef, chicken, fish and seafood

Mattern's Countryside Meats
Phone: (574) 536-2678

Mattern's Butcher Shop and Corner Deli
201 South Main Street; Goshen, IN 46526
Phone: (574) 971-8906

Food allergy information, support and multiple allergy related resources

The Food Allergy & Anaphylaxis Network (FAAN)
11781 Lee Jackson Hwy., Suite 160; Fairfax, VA 22030
Phone: (800) 929-4040
faan@foodallergy.org
www.foodallergy.org

Indiana native Stephanie Hapner has been experimenting with allergen-free food recipes just about forever.

When Stephanie was a junior in high school, she and her father were diagnosed with food allergies. So even before her son Wesley's diagnosis of a rare disease called eosinophilic esophagitis, requiring the removal of numerous food allergens from his diet, Stephanie has endeavored to create recipes that leave behind a host of troubling ingredients without leaving behind the taste. Even as a teen she loved to cook, so though she's received no formal culinary training she's experimented with different food ingredients with the passion of a chemist for nearly 25 years.

Recognized as an expert in allergy-free cooking and wholesome nutrition by doctors and dietitians, Stephanie travels the United States speaking to schools, groups, clubs—wherever people are interested in learning more about recipes using allergy alternatives.

Stephanie and her husband, Brad, reside with their son Wesley in Winona Lake, Indiana.

For more information about Stephanie or her book or to schedule her as a speaker, visit www.stephaniehapner.com.

Wouldn't it be great if **Stephanie** could answer your food allergy questions **daily** or **weekly**?

YOU GOT IT!

One click away at
www.StephanieHapner.com

You'll find:
- Stephanie's allergy-free cooking blog
- Post questions. Get answers.
- Insight and perspective on life with allergies
- Mouth-watering recipes featured
- Cooking tips
- Stephanie's itinerary

LaVergne, TN USA
24 June 2010
187303LV00002B